Ebenezer Weaver Peirce

Historic Sketches

Of Hanson, Lakeville, Mattapoisett, Middleboro', Pembroke, Plympton,

Rochester, etc.

Ebenezer Weaver Peirce

Historic Sketches
Of Hanson, Lakeville, Mattapoisett, Middleboro', Pembroke, Plympton, Rochester, etc.

ISBN/EAN: 9783337143411

Printed in Europe, USA, Canada, Australia, Japan

Cover: Foto ©ninafisch / pixelio.de

More available books at **www.hansebooks.com**

HISTORIC SKETCHES

OF

HANSON, LAKEVILLE, MATTAPOISETT, MIDDLEBORO', PEMBROKE, PLYMPTON, ROCHESTER, WAREHAM, AND WEST BRIDGEWATER.

BY EBENEZER WEAVER PEIRCE,

AUTHOR OF

Brief Sketches of Acushnet, Dighton, Fairhaven, Fall River, Freetown, Somerset, Swanzey and Westport, and Genealogies of the Barnaby, Davis, Peirce, Rounsevill, Strange and Valentine Families, Resident Member of Old Colony Historical, the Pilgrim, and New England Historic Genealogical Societies, Corresponding Member of New York Biographical and Wisconsin State Historical Societies.

"Posterity delight in details."—*John Quincy Adams.*

BOSTON, MASS.
PRINTED FOR THE AUTHOR, BY DEAN DUDLEY,
31 EXCHANGE STREET.
1873

HISTORIC SKETCHES

OF

HANSON, LAKEVILLE, MATTAPOISETT, MIDDLEBORO', PEMBROKE, PLYMPTON, ROCHESTER, WAREHAM, AND WEST BRIDGEWATER.

BY EBENEZER WEAVER PEIRCE,

AUTHOR OF

Brief Sketches of Acushnet, Dighton, Fairhaven, Fall River, Freetown, Somerset, Swanzey and Westport, and Genealogies of the Barnaby, Davis, Peirce, Rounsevill, Strange and Valentine Families. Resident Member of Old Colony Historical, the Pilgrim, and New England Historic Genealogical Societies, Corresponding Member of New York Biographical and Wisconsin State Historical Societies.

"Every particle of historic truth is precious."—*Benjamin Church.*

BOSTON, MASS.

PRINTED FOR THE AUTHOR, BY DEAN DUDLEY,

31 EXCHANGE STREET.

1873.

HISTORY OF FREETOWN.

The author has in manuscript a carefully prepared History of Freetown, with genealogical tables of the families that have resided there at different dates from the purchase of the tract (of the Indians in 1659,) until now. This manuscript furnishes the material for about five hundred pages (large octavo,) and should sufficient encouragement be given will probably ere long be published through the medium of the press. The different subjects treated upon are classified, so as to be easily found and of ready reference, and scarcely any of the matter has ever appeared in print, save about a dozen pages already issued under the title of a "Brief Sketch of Freetown," which of course could convey comparatively few of the facts that go to make up the history of a town that has been settled upon and owned by the white people more than two hundred and ten years.

He has for sale a few copies of the book entitled "The Peirce Family of the Old Colony," a large octavo of five hundred and ten pages, price four dollars; if sent per mail, the postage added.

HISTORY

OF

TOWNS IN PLYMOUTH COUNTY.

HANSON.

This town was detached or set off from Pembroke and incorporated as a new and distinct town in 1820, or about fifty-three years since. Its incorporated limits had formerly been those of a religious parish in Pembroke. and over which, in the gospel ministry, had been ordained and settled Rev. Gad Hitchcock in 1748. He continued to break the bread of life and dispense the word of God among the people of this (then parish now) town for the long term of fifty-five years, and was succeeded in the ministerial office by Rev. George Barstow, who continued in the pastoral relation eighteen years, and died in 1821, aged 51 years. The next minister was Rev. Mr. Howland. Rev. Gad Hitchcock was a finely educated man, a collegian, but better than that he possessed what so many "*book worms*" are wofully deficient in viz , good practical sense, that called "*common sense*," although the most uncommon of all sense existing then, or now extant.

To use the language of one writer concerning the Rev. Mr. Hitchcock "He was sociable, friendly, and hospitable ; esteemed as a man of talents, and many in his old age profited by his instructions."

Many stories are still told of Mr. Hitchcock, that serve to give an idea of his social and even fun loving qualities. The parish that subsequently became a town, by some means acquired the unpoetic name of *Tunk* and Mr. Hitchcock being in company with a sailor, of whom he had asked a great many questions concerning what he had seen and suffered, was by the old tar requested to tell him his name, occupation, and place of residence ; when the reverend gentleman replied, "My name is Gad Hitchcock, I am a minister of the gospel, and preach to the people of Tunk ;" to which the sailor answered, "Gad Hitchcock of Tunk! well, damn me, if I ever before heard such words put together in my life." *

Isaac Peirce,† a soldier in the Narragansett expedition of King Philip's war, is believed to have resided in that part of Pembroke now Hanson. He removed to that part of Middleborough now Lakeville, where he died Feb. 28, 1732, in the 71st, year of his age. His father Abraham Peirce, the emigrant, owned considerable tracts of land in this town. He died in or about 1673.

A company of uniformed militia existed here for several years. It was commanded by Capt. Ebenezer B. K. Gurney, and belonged to the third regiment of Light Infantry, in second Brigade, First Division, Mass. Volunteer Militia, Colonel Eliab Ward, of Middleborough, commanding the Regiment. Brigadier General Henry Dunham, of Abington, the Brigade, and Major General Appleton Howe, of Weymouth, the Division. Capt. Gurney was succeeded by Capt. William H. H. Bryant.

* Rev. Gad Hitchcock served as Chaplain of Col. Thomas Doty's Regiment in 1758. Sergeant Seth Tinkham, clerk of Capt. Benjamin Pratt's company in Col. Doty's Regiment, kept a diary of the marching and fighting done by that regiment, and made several allusions to Rev. Mr. Hitchcock as follows: 1758, August 9. "I went with a party to Load Battoes and heard Mr. Hitchcock preach from Psalms." "Sept. 3d I heard Mr. Hitchcock preach in the Dutch meeting House from Hosea, Chapter 13th, 9th verse."

† Isaac Peirce, the Narragansett Soldier, was ancestor to most the Peirces living in Middleborough and Lakeville. His great grand son Abial Peirce was a captain in the French and Indian War, and Capt. Abial and three brothers or four of one family were captains in the Patriot Army in American Revolution.

TOWN OFFICERS, 1873-4.

Town Clerk. — Josephus Byrant.
Selectmen Assessors, and Overseers of the Poor — E. B. K. Gurney, Joseph B. Howland, Joseph Holmes.
Treasurer and Collector. — Josephus Bryant.
School Committee. — John W. Pratt, Mrs. W. I. Holmes, Otis L. Bonney.
Constables. — Elias C. Poole, Charles C. Wiley, Charles Atwood.
Appropriated $1,500 for schools, $1,300 for the poor, $1,200 for roads, $500 for town officers, $100 for abatement, $1000 for debts, $800 for interest, $300 for incidentals; $7,700.

Unitarian Church.— Meet at Unity Hall, no settled Pastor.
Baptist Church.— Rev. J. B. Reed; Pastor.
Congregational Church.— Rev. S. L. Rockwood, Pastor.
Justices of the Peace — with date of appointment. — Nathaniel Cushing, July 3, 1820; Thomas Hobart, Aug. 28, 1828; Charles Cushing, Feb. 20, 1929; Oliver Whitten, Aug. 27, 1829; Isaac B. Barker, Jan. 6, 1830; Joshua Smith, Oct 1, 1833; David Prouty, Feb 4, 1842; Charles Cushing, Dec. 17, 1842; Thomas Smith, Feb. 9, 1846; Isaiah Bearce, Feb. 26, 1851; Joseph Smith, May. 20, 1856.

LAKEVILLE.

Those readers of current literature who suppose that all the interesting localities of our time-honored commonwealth, have been described and brought into general notice through the medium of that almost universal

"Pen and press, to which we poor mortals owe
All we believe, and almost all we kuow,"

we beg most respectfully to assure of their mistake, and while so doing, to add that there " *yet remaineth*" at least one little town unknown to modern fame, and which has escaped almost all notice from historic, fanciful or sensational writers, in fact the whole family of book-makers, newspaper correspondents and scribblers, and that little town is no more and no less a place than the romantic locality called Lakeville, in the county of Plymouth, and formerly a part of the time-honored old town of Middleborough, Mass.

Middleborough had been settled upon by the white people, passed both in title and occupancy from the aborigines of the soil, and been incorporated as a township, several years prior to the commencement of that greatest and most bloody of New England conflicts, King Philip's War, which by just one century ante-dated the American Revolution, or war for Independence, and that part of ancient Middleborough now Lakeville, was the abode of white men even then.

Lakeville, therefore, as a part of christendom or boasted civilization can claim a history of more than two hundred years, and as part or parts of that history are embraced many important incidents and facts in the details of the several wars in which the country has been engaged.

Going back in the record to the dim and far distant past, and recalling to mind those scenes which preceded and events that ushered in that conflict between races, "King Philip's war," when and where " *The hopes of the Red man perished*," and we find that momentous event the killing of the educated and " Praying Indian" Sausaman occurred upon the soil of Middleborough, and there are good reasons for believing that it was on that part now embraced within the incorporated limits of Lakeville.

Sausaman, leaving the haunts, homes and associations of his brethren the red men his kindred, according to the flesh, sought companionship with the whites, early settlers of Plymouth, and Massachusetts colonies, accepted their religious faith, and gave his attention to books, received instruction in the white man's school or college, in short became civilized and one of a band of christianized heathen, then denominated and known as " *Praying Indians.*"

Returning to the Indians he became a kind of personal or private secretary to the chieftain *Metacom* or King Philip, son of good old Massasoit.

Some difficulty perhaps caused him again to leave the Indians, and seek a home among the white people, whose ears he filled and whose fears he was successful in awakening by mischievious tattling and tale bearing of the plots and plans King Philip was laying and concocting to bring about a war of extermination upon the English, and ridding the country of their presence, cutting off and destroying " *root and branch.*"

This conduct of Sausaman, coming as it did to the ears of King Philip, caused him to seek his destruction, and the indians under orders from their chief, soon found an opportunity of capturing Sausaman, and slaying him.

Fearing the result, should a knowledge of the fact come to the white people, the indians found means to hide the body of Sausaman under the ice of " *Assawamset Pond,*" a very considerable part of which is in Lakeville.

Some English settlers standing upon a bank of the pond witnessed the act of putting the body of Sausaman under the ice, and gave information to the authorities of Plymouth Colony, who visited the spot and recovered the body, which upon examination appeared to have suffered violence and gave convincing proof that death had *not* resulted from drowning.

Several indians were apprehended and charged with the crime of murdering Sausaman, tried by a Jury consisting in part of white men and part indians, and some of those thus charged and tried, were by the Jury found guilty, and by the government of Plymouth Colony, sentenced to suffer death, and executed.

This act of hanging the indians, served effectually to hasten on the terrible war that soon followed, and one of the battles of which was fought upon the soil of Lakeville.

Tipsaquin led the indians, and Capt. Benjamin Church the white people in that battle that was fought upon the southerly bank of "*Assawamset Pond*" near a small stream connecting its waters with those of "*Long Pond*," so called.

A bridge now spans the little stream where that battle was fought, and over which runs the road through that part of the town known as "*Assawamset Neck*" and thence by the old stage route to New Bedford.

It was within that portion of ancient Middleborough now Lakeville, that a reservation of land to the indians was made and occupied and improved by the small remnant of a once powerful tribe for many years.

Amalgamating as the indians did with negroes, the occupants of these reserved lands finally became more African than Native American, and in 1850 or about 23 years ago, report said that only one indian remained, who early the next year lost his life, being drowned in "Assawamset Pond."

The indian reserve is now occupied by negroes, but still retains its name, that by which it has been known for about two hundred years, viz: "*Betty's Neck*"

Thomas Nelson, ancestor of the large and respectable family of that name, purchased lands in Middleborough, now Lakeville, and that part called "Assawamset Neck." This purchase he made in 1714, or about one hundred and sixty years since, and his lands then purchased were bounded on two sides by territory then owned by the indians and reaching entirely across "Assawamset Neck," from the "Assawamset Pond" at one end, to "Long Pond" on the other.

He, with his family, removed to and settled on his purchase in 1717, and these were the first or earliest English settlers upon Assawamset Neck.

Hope Higgins was the maiden name of Mr. Thomas Nelson's wife. She attained to a great age, one hundred and five years and seven months. Eight years before her death she enumerated as her lineal descendants two hundred and fifty-seven persons; and these at her death had increased to about three hundred and thirty-seven. She was interred in the ancient cemetery on the southerly side of Assawamset Pond, and a slate stone bearing an inscription marks her grave. At the date of Mr. Nelson's removal to Assawamset Neck his family consisted of the following named children, born at the dates hereafter mentioned:

Hannah, born April 10, 1699. She married Jabez Wood, Jan. 20, 1719, or two years after coming to reside at Assawamset Neck. Hope, born Dec. 23, 1700. John, born Aug. 1, 1702 married Abiah Leonard Oct. 13, 1726, and he died June 6, 1732. Lois, born Aug. 19, 1704, married Jedediah Thomas March 12, 1724. Ruth, born Feb. 25, 1706, married Henry Thomas Nov. 30, 1726. Elizabeth, born June 3, 1708. Thomas, born April 12, 1710, married Judith Peirce of Middleborough, Dec. 2, 1736. He died March 7, 1768. His wife Judith died Jan. 22, 1792. Sarah, born Aug. 17, 1712. William, born May 20, 1714 married Elizabeth Howland Oct. 2, 1740. Foxell, born June 22, 1716. These ten children were born to Thomas Nelson by Hope his wife, before going to reside upon Assawamset Neck now a part of Lakeville, and two children were born there, viz., Amos, born Dec. 31, 1718, and Ebenezer, born Dec. 22, 1721, or just one hundred and one years after the landing of the Pilgrims at Plymouth.

Mr. Thomas Nelson was one of the earliest, if not indeed the first of those inhabitants of ancient Middleborough who embraced the tenets and doctrines taught by the Calvinistic Baptists. He had been a member of the worshiping congregation and perhaps of the church under the pastoral care and teaching of Rev. Thomas Palmer, second minister of the first Congregational Church in Middleborough, whose habits were such that he was finally deposed from the ministerial office.

Mr. Thomas Nelson discovered such evils in Rev. Mr. Palmer as gave a turn to his mind about religious principles, the final result of which was to cause him to become a Baptist, and ere long to join the first Baptist church in Swanzey, which was the first of that denomination in Massachusetts.

A Baptist church was formed in that part of Middleborough now Lakeville, in 1757, and Rev. Ebenezer Hinds, of Bridgewater, soon after removed thither, and in 1758 was ordained as its pastor. He was succeeded in the ministry by Rev. Simeon Coomb's.

The first meeting house of this Calvinistic Church was removed from the adjoining town of Freetown, that part called New or East Freetown, once Tiverton.

This edifice was accidentally destroyed by fire that also communicated with and burned the parsonage house that stood near.

Another house of worship was erected, but never entirely finished, and becoming somewhat dilapidated, was demolished about thirty years ago.

Their third and last house was commenced in or about 1843, but like the second, was never entirely finished. It was taken down about two years since.

Jabez Wood and wife, Hannah Nelson, were the parents of Rev. Jabez Wood, pastor of the Baptist church in Swanzey.

William Nelson and wife, Elizabeth Howland, were the parents of three Calvinistic Baptist ministers, namely : Rev. William Nelson of Norton, Rev. Samuel Nelson of Raynham, and Rev. Ebenezer Nelson of South Reading, and grandparents of Rev. Ebenezer Nelson Jr., of Lynn.

Thomas Nelson Jr., son of Thomas Nelson and wife, Hope Higgins, was born, as already stated, April 12, 1710, and he became a very useful man in his day, and was of great service to those of his generation, in proof of which it is only necessary to cite the fact that he was elected and served as a Selectman of Middleborough, for the term of twelve years, and for as long a time Moderator of the annual town meeting, and for fourteen years represented that town in the general court at Boston.

Under King George Second, he received the commission of Lieutenant in the fourth company of the local militia of Middleborough, which commission was in 1762 renewed to him under King George Third, Joseph Leonard being at the same time commissioned Captain of the company, and Isaac Peirce, Ensign. This company belonged to the 1st regiment Plymouth County militia.

Lieut. Thomas Nelson Jr., and wife, Judith Peirce, were the parents of John Nelson born Oct. 25, 1737, and who figured quite conspicuously as a patriot in the war of the Revolution.

John Nelson was commissioned a Lieut. of fourth company in Middleborough in or about 1773, promoted to Junior or Second Major of fourth regiment Plymouth county militia, May 9th, 1776 ; Colonel, July first, 1781. He was also for many years one of the Justices of the Peace for that County, and a Selectman of the town of Middleborough. As a Major he served both in Rhode Island and at New Bedford (then Dartmouth) in the war of the Revolution ; Ebenezer Sprout, of Middleborough being his Colonel ; Ebenezer White, of Rochester, Lieut. Colonel ; and Israel Fearing, of Wareham, Senior or First Major.

His wife was Hope, a daughter of Capt. John Rounsevill of East Freetown. Col. John Nelson and Hope Rounsevill were married Nov. 5th, 1760. He died Sept. 11, 1803. She died Dec. 28, 1820, aged 85 years.

Lieut. Thomas Nelson and wife, Judith Peirce, were the grand parents of Hon. Job. Nelson a graduate of Brown University at Providence, R. I., and who studied law and located for practice, at Castine, Me. and in **1804** received the appointment of Judge of Probate for the county of Hancock, that he continued to hold until 1836, a period of about **32** years. Judge **Nelson** died July second, 1850. Judge **Nelson** was a brother of Rev. Stephen S. Nelson, a Calvinistic Baptist minister at Attleborough.

The late Job Peirce Nelson, Esq., was also a lineal desendant of Thomas Nelson and wife, Hope **Higgins**, through their son Lieut. Thomas Nelson and wife, Judith Peirce, grandson Thomas Nelson and wife, Anna Smith, and great grandson Deacon Abial Nelson and wife, Sally Peirce.

Job Peirce Nelson was born in Middleborough, now Lakeville, Oct. 17, 1806, joined in marriage with Fatima Baker of Upton, Mass. Oct. 9, 1834, and died Dec. 3, 1862. He was mainly instrumental in effecting the division of the town of Middleborough, and setting off a part as a new and distinct town, the voters of the part thus set off, by a handsome majority in open town meeting, deciding should be incorporated under the name of *Nelson*, in token of their respect for the subject of this notice, but which his modesty led him to oppose and discourage, when the name of Lakeville that it now bears was substituted for that of Nelson. He was a justice of Peace for Plymouth County, was born, lived and died on the farm purchased by his great great grand father, Thomas Nelson in 1714, and a part of which had descended to him as a birthright through the successive generations that had owned, occupied and improved, (but never sold) it, for a term of one hundred and forty-eight years, and that still remains as the home of his children.

The Congregational Church in Lakeville was formed in or about 1724, and Rev. Benjamin Ruggles ordained Pastor. He here continued in the work of the gospel ministry about thirty years and was succeeded by Reverend Caleb Turner who was ordained in 1761. Rev. Mr. Crafts succeeded Mr. Turner and then the pulpit was for several years filled by Rev. John Shaw. This church and society have had three meeting houses. The third and last house is that now occupied, and was built about 37 years since.

A religious association called "*United Brethren*," was formed in that part of Middleborough now Lakeville, about eighty years ago. This association was subsequently organized as a church, and known as the Fourth Baptist Church in Middleborough.

Their place of worship was the "Pond Meeting House" so called that stood on the southerly bank of Assawamset Pond, and erected in or about 1796. Destroyed by fire in 1870.

The Christian denomination erected a church edifice on "*Mullain Hill*" so called, about thirty years since, that is still occupied as a place of worship by the Christian church and society of Lakeville.

The "*Free Will Baptists*" have a meeting house in which they never meet. It stands in that part of the town called "Beach woods," and though comparatively a new house is in a very dilapidated condition.

Isaac Peirce, a soldier in the Narragansett expedition of King Philip's war, died in that part of Middleborough now Lakeville, Feb. 28, 1732, in his 71st, year. He must have have been born in or about 1661. Was a son of Abraham Peirce, the emigrant, who arrived at Plymouth in 1623, and died in Duxbury in or about 1673.

Isaac Peirce Jr., a Quaker, settled in town in or about 1709 and died here Jan. 17, 1757. He, with Benj. Booth, purchased a large tract of land lying in Taunton and Lakeville, (then Middleborough) January 23, 1709, being the date of the deed.

The wife of Isaac Peirce Jr., was Judith, a daughter of John Booth of Scituate, Mass. She was born March 13, 1680, and died May 4, 1733.

Abial Peirce, (a grand son of Isaac Peirce Jr., and great grand son of Isaac Peirce the veteran soldier of King Philip's war), was born in that part of Middleborough now Lakeville, Sept. 10, 1733. As a private soldier he served in the expedition to Acadia for the removal of the neutral French or Acadians in Sept. 1755, and re-enlisted into the army July 15, 1756, served in a company commanded by Capt, Samuel N. Nelson. Continuing in the service, he was made a Corporal, and on the fourth of May 1759, a Lieut. and as a commissioned officer, he took part in the battle at Quebec, Sept. 13, 1759, being an eye witness to the fall and death of Gen. Wolfe. The next year Lieut. Abial Peirce was made a captain in the army of the frontier, and performed a tour of duty in the field, his company being a part of Col. Willard's Regt. Capt. Abial Peirce in the capacity of a private soldier, a corporal, lieut. and capt. was imperiling his life in the battle field during most of the time intervening between the summer of 1755, and the treaty of peace concluded and signed at Paris. Feb. 10, 1763.

Twelve years later, the veteran captain of the "French and Indian war" promptly responded to the "*first call*" of his oppressed and bleeding country, leading one of the five com-

OLD FARM HOUSE OF CAPT. JOB PEIRCE, TAKEN DOWN IN 1870.

panies of Middleborough, which took the field on the 19th of April 1775, amid the stirring scenes of Lexington and Concord. On the rolls at the State House, Capt. Abial Peirce's company is called the second company in Middleborough.

As a large part of that company resided within the present limits of Lakeville, the names of its several members properly should be made to constitute, as it really is, a part of the revolutionary history of that town, and hence we here present a copy of the roll of Captain Abial Peirce's company of *Minute Men*, as the same appears in the archives of the Secretary of State, at Boston.

Abial Peirce. Captain ; Joseph Macomber, First Lieut. ; Benjamin Darling, Second Lieut. ; Josiah Smith, Richard Peirce, Elias Miller jr., and Job Macomber, Sergeants ; Bachellor Bennett, Jedediah Lyon, Samuel Eddy, and John Bly, Corporals ; Caleb Simmons, Drummer ; and Nathaniel Foster, Fifer.

Private Soldiers. Job Peirce, Samuel Hoar, David Thomas second, Michael Mosher, Jesse Pratt, Jacob Hayford, Job Hunt, Henry Bishop, Consider Howland, Noah Clark, Corneilus Haskins, John Rogers, Lebbeus Simmons, Caleb Wood, John Booth, Ithamer Haskins, John Reynolds, Nathaniel Macomber, Levi Jones, Josiah Smith jr., Malachi Howland jr., Zachariah Paddock, jr., Rufus Howland, Silva Purrington, John Fry, jr., John Douglas, jr., Ebenzer L. Bennett, Samuel Miller, Isaac Canedy, Daniel Reynolds, Rufus Weston, Ziba Eaton, Isaac Miller, Nehemiah Peirce, Samuel Bennett, Joshua Thomas, Calvin Johnson, Joshua Read, Cryspus Shaw, James Willis, Sylvanus Churchill, Samuel Macomber, Richard Omey, Israel Thomas, Ichabod Read, Samuel Ransom and Daniel Jucket.

When men were enlisted for a longer term of time, and the necessities of the the case required the raising of a Continental Army, Captain Abial Peirce enlisted another company, consisting of sixty-nine men, of whom five belonged in Abington, twenty-five in Bridgewater, twenty-five in Middleborough, ten in Rochester, and four in Wareham. This company was a part of Colonel Dike's regiment, on duty for a time at or near Boston. Captain Abial Peirce died Dec. 26, 1811. He was buried in South Middleborough, but no stone bearing an inscription tells where he lies.

Job Peirce (a brother of Captain Abial Peirce and great grand son of the Narragansett Soldier), was born in what is now Lakeville, Nov. 29, 1737, and as a private soldier performed a short tour of duty in a company of the local militia (commanded by Captain Joseph Tinkham), upon an alarm in 1757, occasioned by an attack made by the French upon Fort William Henry.

In the war between England and France, that quickly followed, and which in this country acquired the name of " French and Indian War," Job Peirce faithfully and honorably served out three enlistments, dated April 5, 1758, April 6, 1759, and March 24, 1762, receiving his final discharge at the termination of the war. While serving on the first of these enlistments, he was a soldier in Captain Benjamin Pratt's company of Colonel Doty's Regiment, and participated in the disastrous attempt to take Ticonderoga from the French, in which, added to other very serious losses sustained by the English, their intrepid and popular leader Lord Howe was killed.

His second enlistment was passed on duty in Nova Scotia, and at its close he took passage on board a government transport, bound for Boston, but encountering a severe storm they were driven far off the coast, and reduced to an almost unmanageable wreck, that at the mercy of the waves drifted about until the passengers and crew were on the verge of starvation, when they succeeded in reaching land, upon one of the West India Islands.

So long was his absence prolonged, that his parents had given him up, and mourned for him as dead, when one Sabbath morning during religious service at the church, they were overjoyed to see him enter the house and take a seat in their family pew, having reached home soon after the family had left home to attend the services of the sanctuary.

From the close of the French and Indian War, to the commencement of the war af the Revolution, a period of about twelve years, Job Peirce was industriously engaged in the avocation and labors of a farmer, and realizing the truth of that proverb, " *the hand of the diligent maketh rich.*"

The tocsin of war sounding the " *Lexington Alarm*," so called, had no sooner reached his ear, than like Putnam, he

" Left his ploughshare in the mold,
Flocks and herds without a fold,
And mustered in his simple dress
For wrongs to seek, a stern redress ;
To right those wrongs, come weal, come woe,
To perish or o'ercome the foe."

In the company of " *Minute Men*," (commanded by his brother Captain Abial Peirce), Job Peirce served as a private soldier, and in the early attempts to raise a continental army

Job Peirce was commissioned Second Lieutenant, and served at Roxbury, in a company commanded by Captain Nathaniel Wood, it being a part of Colonel Simeon Carey's regiment.

May 9, 1776, Job Peirce was promoted to Captain, and the next year commanded a company of 93 men in Colonel Theopholus Cotton's regiment, on duty in Rhode Island, the "*secret expedition*," so called.

He was also in the field, and helped to repel the British soldiers and frustrate their attempt to burn the village of Fairhaven, September 17, 1778.

Twas not alone as a soldier, brave, self-denying, and patient in the endurance of hardship, that Job Peirce acquired the esteem, love and respect of those with whom he had to do, for his were the triumphs of peace as much, and perhaps even more, than those of war. His courage in war was not exceeded by his good conduct in peace, for he was ever " diligent in business, serving the Lord," and both by precept and example, ever exercising a healthfull moral and religious influence. To religious and benevolent enterprises his heart and hands were always open, and no other man of his time in Middleborough, bestowed so much money on objects of charity. He was the donor of Peirce Academy. He died July 22, 1819.

Henry Peirce, a brother of Captains Abial and Job Peirce, was born in that part of Middleborough now Lakeville, in or about 1743, and at an early age imbibing the military spirit of his brothers, enlisted into the army and performed a tour of duty in the field when only seventeen years of age.

This his first tour of duty was performed in Captain Abial Peirce's company, of Colonel Willard's Regiment.

March 24, 1762, Henry Peirce, commenced upon the duties of a second enlistment, and in the company of Capt. Ephraim Holmes, in which command his brother Job Peirce served at the same time.

Their services closed with the ending of that war terminated by the treaty of peace concluded at Paris, in France, Feb. 10, 1763. At the " Lexington Alarm," April 19, 1775, Henry Peirce served in the company of " Minute Men" commanded by Capt. Isaac Wood, of Middleborough, and repaired to Marshfield, to administer a quietus to those people of that town who had banded together under the name of "*Associated Loyalists.*" He soon after assisted Captain Levi Rounsevill of Freetown, in raising a company for Colonel Brewer's regiment, in Patriot army of Revolution, in which company he received the commission of a Lieutenant.

Capt. Rounsevill's company was enlisted in the towns of Freetown, Dartmouth, and Middleborough, and as some of those enlisted in the town last named, resided in that part now Lakeville, we give the Middleborough list entire. Lieut. Henry Peirce; Sergeants, Joseph Macomber, Job Hunt and David Trouant; Corporals, Hilkiah Peirce, and Richard Peirce; Drummer, Leonard Hinds; Privates, William Armstrong, Joseph Booth, Ephraim Douglas, Henry Evans, Anthony Fry, Levi Simmons, and Nathan Trouant.

At Rhode Island, in 1777, Henry Peirce, who had been promoted to a Capt. commanded a company in Colonel Theopholus Cotton's regiment, and several of this company lived in what is now Lakeville. Capt. Henry Peirce's company on that tour of duty consisted of the following named persons. Henry Peirce, Captain; Peter Hoar, Lieutenant; and George Shaw, Ensign. Non Commissioned Officers; Amasa Wood, Daniel Ellis, Joseph Wood, Roland Leonard, Geo. Hackett, William Hall, James Le Baron, Nathaniel Cole, Israel Eaton, and Haziel Purrinton.

Private Soldiers: Churchill Thomas, Jeremiah Thomas, Andrew Cobb, Samuel Sampson, James Palmer, Elijah Shaw, David Fish, Jacob Soule, Hazael Tinkham, Jabez Vaughn, Samuel Barrows, Joseph Bennett, John Morton, John Morton, 2nd, Roland Smith, Rounsevill Peirce, Peter Thomas, Edmund Weston, Joseph Tupper, Lemuel Lyon, William Littlejohn, Daniel Cox, Thomas Pratt, David Pratt, Abia, Booth, Ebenezer Howland, Josiah Kingman, Jacob Perkins, Luther Pratt, Seth Wade, Noah Haskell, Lemuel Raymond, Manasseh Wood, Francis Le Baron, Asaph Churchill, Samuel Thomas, Nathaniel Thomas, Edward Washburn, William Bly, Joseph Macomber, Lemuel Briggs, Jonathan Wescott, Ephraim Dunham, Isaac Harlow, Nathaniel Cobb, Andrew Ricket, Jonathan Porter, James Porter, James Sprout, and John Thrasher. Commissoned 3, Non-Commissioned, and Musicians 10, Privates 50. Total, 63.

About three years later viz., in the month af Aug. 1780, Capt. Henry Peirce was again on duty in Rhode Island, commanding a company in the regiment led by Lieut. Colonel Ebenezer White, of Rochester, the members of which company were nearly, if indeed not quite all residents of what is now Lakeville, and whose names were as follows: Henry Peirce, Captain; Peter Hoar, Lieut.; Ezra Clark, Ensign. Non-commissioned Officers; Ebenezer Hinds, Robert Hoar, Joseph Booth, Nathaniel Macomber, Benjamin Booth, Henry Edminster, and Ebenezer Hayford. Private Soldiers, Josiah

Holloway, Ezra Reynolds, John Reynolds, Benjamin Reynolds, Elections Reynolds, Isaac Reynolds, Enos Reynolds, Ebenezer Howland, Samuel Howland, John Howland, Joshua Howland, Eseck Howland, John Hoar, John Holloway, Richard Parris, Samuel Parris, Uriah Peirce, George Peirce, Seth Simmons, Lebeus Simmons, Jacob Sherman, Earl Sears, Nathan Trouant, Daniel Collins, John Church, and Roger Clark.

At the reorganization of the miltia consequent upon the adoption of a State constitution, Capt. Henry Peirce was commissioned by Gov. John Hancock, to command a company of the local militia in Middleborough, (that called the "*Seventh company*," or more) familiarly known as "*Beach Woods Company*." As all this company was included within the present limits of Lakeville, we give a copy of the names borne upon its roll, both of "*train band* and *alarm list*," as a means of determining who were "able bodied white male citizens" of this locality, 92 years ago.

Train Band.

Henry Peirce, Captain ; Peter Hoar, Lieut. ; Robert Hoar, William Canedy, Bradock Hoar,———— Howland, Sergeants ; Lebbeus Simmons, Seth Simmons, Corporals ; Stephen Hathaway, James Peirce, Enos Peirce, George Peirce, Simeon Peirce, Seth Keen, Joseph Keen, Philip Haskins, Josiah Holloway, John Allen, Samuel Parris, Isaac Parris, Moses Parris, Seth Borden, William Strobridge, John Haskins, John Thrasher, Joseph Booth, Benjamin Booth, Ebenezer Hafford, Barnabas Clark, Samuel Record, Isaac Smith, Jonathan Hafford. Samuel Howland, Henry Edminster, Consider Howland, Ebenezer Howland, Rufus Howland, Eseck Howland, John Hoar, William Hoar, Isaac Hathaway, David Pratt, Seth Ramsdell, Jacob Sherman, and David Bramin, Private Soldiers.

Alarm List.

Daniel Jucket, Joseph Booth, Josiah Smith, Nathaniel Clossen, Job Chase, Ezra Clark, Richard Peirce, and Abraham Peirce. Train Band, 45 ; Alarm List, 8 ; Total, 53.

Captain Henry Peirce died Jan. 22, 1791, and his remains were interred in the ancient cemetery, on the southerly border of Assawamset Pond, his grave being marked by suitable stones bearing inscriptions.

Seth Peirce, a brother of Captains Abial, Job, and Henry Peirce, was born in Middleborough now Lakeville, in or about 1747. At the "Lexington Alarm," he served in a company commanded by Captain Nathaniel Wood, which command, upon the records at the State House in Boston, appears under the title of First Company of militia in Middleborough. The local militia of that town then existed in the form of four companies, of which the first and second responded at the *first call*, or "Lexington Alarm," as it came to be called. Removing to Shutesbury, in Hampshire (now Franklin, County, while the war of the revolution was progressing, he was commissioned Captain of a company raised for the Patriot army, and from enlistments in the towns of Leverett, Northfield, New Salem, and Shutesbury, and consisting of 75 men, with which he repaired to the fields of revolutionary strife.

July 1, 1781, Capt. Seth Peirce was commissioned to command a company of the local miltia of Shutesbury, and was a Selectman of that town four years. His last years were spent at Hardwick, in Worcester county, which town he represented in the general court in 1806. He married four times. He died February 25, 1809. Was buried in Hardwick, and has suitable grave stones.

Ebenezer Peirce, another brother of the foregoing Capttains Abial, Job, Henry, and Seth Peirce, lost his life while serving as a private soldier in the Patriot army of the American Revolution, being on duty at Newport, Rhode Island.

Few families in any part of our country can show so patriotic a record. Of a family of six sons, all were engaged in fighting the battles of the revolution, four attaining not only to the rank and commissions, but exercising the command of Captains, on the battle-field, and one sacrificing his life for his country, and neither of the surviving five (four of whom had served the country as soldiers in two wars), received or applied for a pension from the government.

Nor did this spirit of true manliness, uncommon devotion to noble principles and love of conntry die with that generaation, but was in some good degree transmitted to their posterity, inhabiting this and other towns of this State, and even to children's children, now residing at the far West. Capt. Abial Peirce's oldest son, William Peirce, born in Middleborough, June 2, 1759, removed to the State of New York, and lost his life while serving in the army in the late war with England, sometimes called the war of 1812. He died Nov. 5, 1812, and consequently must have been more than fifty years of age, not liable to draft or service in the militia, and therefore a volunteer in the arduous enterprise that cost him his life.

A great grand son of Capt. Abial Peirce, who bears up and honors both the given and surname, removed to the State of Iowa, where he was elected to a seat in the Legislature, which place he promptly resigned, that he might respond to the "first call" for soldiers, in the late war of the Rebellion. He was made Captain of Cavalry, and in the battle of "Pea Ridge" had a horse shot from under him.

June 20, 1863, Capt. Abial R. Peirce, of 4th regiment Iowa cavalry, was promoted to Major, and in the performance of the duties of which office he had five horses shot under him. Since the war, he has been elected to the Senate of Iowa.

That alarm of April 19, 1775, found the veteran captain of the "French and Indian War," at his plow in the peaceful fields of agriculture, in the ancient old colony town of Middleborough, while that of April 19, 1861, eighty-six years later, was sounded in the ears of his great grand son, occupying a seat in the Legislative hall, of a new and rapidly growing State, and with the same alacrity that the former relinquished his agricultural pursuits, did the latter resign his office as a legislator, with its safety and ease, honors and emoluments, and in worthy imitation of former, hasten to respond to the *first call* of his bleeding country.

William R. Peirce, oldest son of Capt. Job Peirce, was born in Middleborough, April 19, 1764, and was consequently eleven years of age, the day that the soils of Lexington, and Concord, were wet with the first blood of the Revolution, and although only eighteen at the close of that war, yet had he served as a soldier in the Patriot army, at Rhode Island, and as a sailor in the Patriot navy, was captured, carried to England, and confined as a prisoner of war, and liberated at the declaration of peace. Became a master mariner, and died on the Island of Saint Bartholemew, May 15, 1794.

Job Peirce, second son of Captain Job Peirce, was born in Middleborough now Lakeville, Dec. 12, 1767; on attaining to manhood he went to Assonet Village, in Freetown, where he engaged largely and very successfully in merchandise and ship building, and was noted for his great liberality, and benevolence. Died Sept. 22, 1805, and was buried with military honors by the military company, of which he held the commission of Captain, at the time of his decease.*

---

* Job Peirce, jr., was commissioned Captain of the first company in the local militia of Freetown, Aug. 21, 1801, and held that office until his death, Sept. 22, 1805. Although never a professor of religion, he was mainly instrumental in establishing the Christian denomination in Freetown, a sect now the most numerous of any in that place. He was Town clerk in 1802, and Auditor of the town accounts in 1803.

Former Residence of Capt. Job Peirce, Jr., in Freetown.

Levi, third son, born Oct. 1, 1773, (was named for his mother's brother, Captain Levi Rounsevill, Capt. of Minute Men, of Freetown, and also Captain in Continental army), Levi Peirce was commissioned Major of fourth Regiment in Plymouth County Brigade, June 8, 1809, Senior Major in 1812.* Honorably dischaged in 1816. Commanded a Battalion of the coast guard in last war with England. Member of Constitutional Convention, 1820. Post master, and Justice of the Peace. The following is copied from his tomb stone :

"Deacon Levi Peirce, died Aug. 22, 1847, aged 74 years. At his own expense, he built the meeting house of the Central Baptist Church, in Middleborough, and liberally endowed it, and remained Deacon of the same, from the time of its formation, till his death, a term of twenty years, using the office of Deacon well. The righteous shall be had in everlasting remembrance."

Peter Hoar Peirce, seventh son of Captain Job Peirce, was born March 25, 1788, died Jan. 27, 1861. He was a member of Mass. Senate, Justice of Peace, and Coroner, Capt. of militia from Feb. 18, 1814, Major, 1816, Lieut. Colonel, April 25, 1817, honorably discharged 1823.

In the last war with England, he commanded a company of the coast guard, stationed at or near Plymouth. As a part of that company resided in what is now Lakeville, we give the roll entire. Peter H. Peirce, Captain; Luther Murdock, Lieutenant; Orrin Tinkham, Ensign; Thomas Bump, Hercules Richmond, George Shaw, Ezra Wood, and Ichabod Wood, Sergeants; Daniel Hathaway, Andrew Warren, Abner Leonard, and Daniel Thomas, Corporals; Oliver Sharp, and Paddock Tinkham, Musicians; Jeremiah Wood, Levi Wood, Cyrenus Tinkham, Gideon Leonard, Peter Vaughn, Jos. Clark, Edmund Ellis, Eliphalet Doggett, Oliver L. Sears, Nathan Perkins, Josiah D. Burgess, Joseph Waterman, Isaac Thomas jr., Joshua Atwood jr., Andrew McCully, Daniel Norcut, Seth Weston, Abel Howard, Ben. Leonard, Cyrus White, Beniah Wilder, Levi Thomas, second, Calvin

---

* The office of Senior Major, to which Levi Peirce was promoted in 1812, was the same, and required of him the performance of precisely the duties now devolving upon a Lieutenant Colonel. A militia regiment, was then commanded by a Lieutenant Colonel Commandant, and the other field officers were a Senior Major, and Junior Major When Levi Peirce, was Senior Major of 4th Regiment, his brother-in-law, Abial Washburn was Lieut. Colonel Commandant, and Ephraim Ward, second Major or Junior Major. On the resignation of Levi Peirce, Ephraim Ward succeeded him as Senior Major, and Peter H Peirce, was promoted from the office of Capt. to that of Junior Major.

Dunham, Caleb Tinkham, Abraham **Thomas** jr., **Rufus** Alden, jr., Daniel Weston, Joseph Paddock, Nathaniel Macomber, William Ramsdell, John C. Perkins, Edward Winslow jr., Isaac Cobb, Thomas C. Ames, Unite Kinsley, Levi Haskins, George Ellis, Cornelius Tinkham, Samuel Cole, Thomas Southworth, Daniel Vaughn, Cushman Vaughn, Sylvanus T. Wood, Cyrus Nelson, Augustus Bosworth, Lorenzo Wood, Jacob Bennett second, Andrew Bump, Josephus Bump, Nathan Reed, Benejeh Peirce, William Littlejohn jr., Warren Bump jr., Francis Billington jr., Joseph Standish, Earl Bourne, George Caswell jr., Israel Keith, Sylvanus Vaughn, Leonard Southworth, Elisha Shaw, William Cole, James Cole, Rodolfus Barden, and Sylvanus Barrows, Privates.

Beside the Nelson and Peirce families, among the early settlers of what is now Lakeville, was the Hoars, who probably came from Taunton. Samuel Hoar married Rebecca Peirce, a daughter of Isaac Peirce, the soldier in Narragansett War. The children of Samuel Hoar and wife Rebecca, were Samuel, born Aug. 12, 1716, died April 5, 1736, Robert, born May 23, 1719, married Sarah Willis, of Bridgewater, she died January 13, 1753, and he for a second wife married Judith Tinkham, of Middleborough, Oct. 4, 1753, and she died Feb. 26, 1761. For a third wife he married Rachel Hoskins, Feb. 26, 1761.

William, born Dec. 30, 1721, married Jan. 31, 1745, Sarah Hoskins, of Taunton, she was a daughter of Henry Hoskins of Taunton, a blacksmith, and born of his wife, Abigail Godfrey, and a grand-daughter of William Hoskins, of Taunton, a soldier in the Narragansett war. William Hoar, was deacon of the Calvinistic Baptist Church, herein noticed, of which the Rev. Mr. Hinds, was the first pastor. Deacon William Hoar, died April 25, 1795. Sarah, his wife, died Nov. 15, 1774. They were the parents of Braddock Hoar, a patriot soldier in the war for Independence, and who afterward removed to the State of New York. Peter Hoar, a Patriot officer in the war of American Revolution, was a son of Robert Hoar, and born of his second wife, Judith Tinkham.

At the Lexington alarm, Peter Hoar served as a private soldier, in a company of Minute Men, commanded by Capt. Isaac Wood, and next as a Sergeant in Captain Job Peirce's company, on duty in Rhode Island, and being promoted to Lieut. served under Capt. Henry Peirce, at Rhode Island, (Col. Cotton's Regiment), in 1777, and Lieut. Col. White's regiment, in 1780. He also performed duty in the field as

Lieut. of Capt Edward Sparrows' company, in Col. Tyler's regiment. At the reorganization of local militia in 1781, he was commissioned Lieut. of the 7th company in Middleborough, and promoted to Capt. of 2d company, June 6, 1793, Junior Major of 4th regiment in Plymouth County Brigade, in 1797, Senior Major, July 22, 1800, honorably discharged, in 1806. He died March 12, 1815, aged sixty years. Was a Selectman of the town of Middleborough, fifteen years; Representative to general court, three years, and a Justice of Peace from 1811, until his death. Distinguished for his generosity, liberality, and benevolence.

The 7th company in the local militia of Middleborough, having been entirely within the limits of Lakeville, a list of its successive commanders properly constitutes a part of the history of this town.

Capt. Henry Peirce, from July 1, 1781, to 1787; James Peirce, from July 17, 1787, to 1796; Abanoam Hinds, from 1796, to 1802; Elkanah Peirce, from May 4, 1802, to 1807; Elisha Briggs, from 1807, to 1811; Sylvanus Parris, from March 20, 1811, to 1815; Ethan Peirce, from June 6, 1815, to 1822; Apollos Reed, from 1822, to 1827; John Strobridge, from May 19, 1827, to 1829; Samuel Hoar, from June 6, 1829, to May 30, 1831; Silas P. Ashley, from 1831, to 1837.

A large part of the 4th company in Middleborough, was in what is now Lakeville, and its commanders were as follows.

Joseph Leonard, from 1759, to 1773; William Canedy jr., from 1773, to Sept. 19, 1775; Job Peirce, from May 9, 1776, to 1778; Amos Washburn, from 1778, to 1781; Abraham Shaw, from July 1, 1781, to 17—; John Smith, from 178—; Ebenezer Briggs, from Aug. 4, 1794, Elias Sampson Ebenezer Pickens, from 1807, to 1814; David Sherman, from May 3, 1814, to 1821; Abial Sampson, from 1821, to 1826; Richard B. Foster, from 1826, to 1828; Horatio G. Clark, from July 19, 1828, to Jan. 23, 1829; James Pickens, from May 29, 1829, to May 30, 1830 when the 4th company was disbanded, and the members enrolled in the 7th company, then under Capt. Samuel Hoar.

The following named gentlemen residing within the limits of Lakeville, held commissions, in the militia higher than that of Captain.

BRIGADIER GENERAL.—Ephraim Ward, from January 27, 1825, to 1828.

COLONELS.—John Nelson, from July 1, 1781, to 1787. Ephraim Ward, April 25, 1817, to January 27, 1825.

LIEUTENANT COLONELS. — Peter Hoar, from July 22, 1800, to 1806, Ephraim Ward, from 1816, to April 25, 1817, Ebenezer W. Peirce, from April 3, 1852, to Nov. 7, 1855.

MAJORS. — Elkanah Leonard, 17—; John Nelson, from May 9, 1776, to July 1, 1781; Peter Hoar, from Jan. 4, 1797, to July 22, 1800; Ephraim Ward, from 1812, to 1816; Harry Jackson, from January 29, 1823, to 1823; Ebenezer W. Peirce, Aug. 1851, to April 3, 1852.

Names of gentlemen born in that part of Middleborough, now Lakeville, and who held military commissions higher than that of Captain, after going to reside elsewhere.

BRIGADIER GENERAL. — Abial Washburn, from September 4, 1816, to Dec. 1824.

COLONEL. — Abial Washburn, from July 22, 1800, to Sept. 4, 1816; Edward G. Perkins, from 1837, to 1839.

LIEUTENANT COLONELS. — Abial Washburn, from Jan. 4, 1797, to July 22, 1800; Levi Peirce, from 1812. to 1816; Peter Hoar Peirce, from April 25, 1817, to 1823; Edward G. Perkins, from May 7, 1834, to 1837.

MAJOR. — Abial Washburn, from May 1, 1794, to Jan. 4, 1797; Levi Peirce, from June 8, 1809, to 1812; Peter H. Peirce, from 1816, to April 25, 1817; George Ward, from May 1850, to 1851.

Names of gentlemen who were residents of Lakeville, and received commissions higher than that of Captain, after going to live elsewhere.

BRIGADIER GENERAL. — Eliab Ward, from April 1850, to Oct. 1855; Ebenezer W. Peirce, from Nov. 7. 1855, to Dec. 13, 1861; when he received the appointment of Colonel in the army

COLONEL. — Eliab Ward, from July 10 1844, to April 1850.

LIEUTENANT COLONEL. — Eliab Ward, from Aug. 1843, to July 10, 1844.

Justices of the Peace — in time past and present. — Elkanah Leonard, John Nelson, Peter Hoar, Abial P. Booth, Abner Clark, Oliver Peirce, Thomas Doggett, Job P. Nelson, Luther Washburn, Abizah T. Harvey, Reuben Hafford, Jirch Winslow, Job Peirce, Harrison Staples, Churchill T. Westgate W. H. Southworth.

Coroner — Ebenezer W. Peirce, appointed Jan. 7, 1854.

First list of town officers, elected immediately after the incorporation of the town in 1853.

Selectmen and Assessors — Reuben Hafford Esq., Ezra McCulley, and Nathaniel Sampson.

Overseers of the Poor — Eleazer Richmond, Job Peirce, and Ebenezer W. Peirce.
Clerk and Treasurer — Isaac Sampson.
Constable — Churchill T. Westgate.

TOWN OFFICERS, 1873.

Moderator — W. H. Southworth.
Town Clerk, Treasurer and Collector — C. T. Westgate.
Selectmen and Assessors — Leonard Washburn, Sydney T. Nelson, James P. Peirce.
Overseers of the Poor — Eleazer Richmond, James P. Peirce, Job Peirce.
School Committee for three years — Henry L. Williams, Mrs. Job Peirce, E. W. Barrows.
Auditor — Uriah Sampson.
Constables — John Cudworth, John Dean, H. B. Coombs.
Fence Viewers — Leonard Washburn, S. T. Nelson, James P. Peirce.
Fish Wardens — John Cudworth, John Dean, H. B. Coombs.
Field Drivers and Pound Keepers — P. C. Dean, J. P. Peirce, O. S. Robbins, W. Canedy, J. Cummings, B. H. Reed, W. A. Coombs, S. T. Nelson, E. Richmond, Charles Shockley, John Meack, Jireh Winslow, John Shaw, S. D. Pickens.
Surveyors of Highway — Leonard Washburn, A. C. Southworth, J. H. Nelson, E. W. Williams, S. T. Nelson, Lewis Parris, Leander Winslow, Simeon Baker, John Allen, H. L. Williams, J. M. Godfrey, J. E. Ashley,
Surveyors of Wood, Bark and Lumber — Charles R. Richmond, Cephas Haskins, James P. Peirce, John Cudworth, John F. Allen, Leander Winslow, Enos Peirce, Job T. Tobey.
Keeper of Town Pound — Abram Shaw.
Justices of the Peace — with date of their appointment.— Job P. Nelson, May 14, 1851; Reuben Hafford, May 14, 1851; Thomas Doggett, Jan 4, 1853; Harrison Staples, May 31, 1856.
Voted to raise the sum of $3200 for the support of schools and to defray town expenses, and $1300 for the repair of Highways.
Congregational Church at Precinct — No settled Pastor.
Christian Church — No settled Pastor.
Lakeville Library Association — Rooms at N. Miller Sampson's, J. F. Montgomery, President.

The Lakeville Post Office is near the depot of the O. C. & N. R. R.; Cephas Haskins, Esq., Postmaster.

No Post of the Grand Army in Lakeville. Members of that association residing here generally belong to the Ebenezer W. Peirce Encampment, or Post 8, Middleborough, and of which, for the present year, Job Morton Staples, of Lakeville, is Commander.

MATTAPOISETT.

Mattapoisett is a word from the Indian language, and said to signify rest.

Indians living a few miles back from the seaboard, used frequently to come down to the shore at this place for the purpose of obtaining fish and clams, and at an adjacent spring stopped to rest, and hence the name that they gave that locality, the river, and some of the surrounding country.

Mattapoisett was formerly a religious parish in Rochester, set off as such during the ministry of Rev. Timothy Ruggles, and settling as their minister, Rev. Ivory Hovey, who in 1722, was succeeded by Rev. Lemuel Le Baron. These two gentlemen ministered in things spiritual to the people at this place for the full term of a century. Their next minister, was Rev. Thomas Robbins, D. D. who was believed to be the owner of the most valuable private library in the State. For further information concerning this library, see *Rochester*.

Ship building formerly formed an important branch of business at this place, as did also the whale fishery, but both are now nearly or quite relinquished.

Rogers L. Barstow, Esq., an enterprising merchant, was largely interested in the whale fishery up to the time of death.

As a business man Major Barstow, is greatly missed, and his death may justly be considered a great loss to the town, indeed a public misfortune, for as a public spirited citizen, " *he was a man take him all in all, whose like*" the people of this community will not probably soon possess as a neighbor, counsellor, and friend, or his equal in business capacity, " *to look upon again.*"

Major Barstow, was nearly or quite a " *teetotaler*" in practice, if not in principle. Ardent spirits he neither tasted, touched, or handled.

He was mainly instrumental in getting up a Light Infantry company, at this place, in 1842, and of which he was the first captain, with Loring Meigs, John T. Atsatt, and David Pratt as Lieutenants.

This company belonged to the Bristol County Battalion, then composed of the "*Norton Artillery,*" "*Cohanet Rifle Corps,*" of Taunton, "*New Bedford Guards,*"* and "*Mattapoisett Guards.*" The Battallion was commanded by Major Benjamin R. Gulliver, of Taunton ; Captain Barstow next received the appointment as Quarter Master on the Brigade Staff of General Henry Dunham, of Abington.

A few years later Captain Barstow was promoted to the office of Major of the third regiment of Light Infantry, Stephen Thomas of Middlborough, being Colonel, and Ebenezer W. Peirce of Lakeville, Lieutenant Colonel.

Major Rogers L. Barstow, was elected a Representative to the General Court at Boston, and commissioned a Justice of the Peace for Plymouth County.

Probably the first or earliest company of light infantry raised in that part of Rochester now *Mattapoisett*, was authorised by the following order :

"COMMONWEALTH OF MASSACHUSETTS. — The Committee of the Council on Military Affairs, to whom was referred the petition of Ebenezer Barrows and others, representing that the village of Mattapoisett, in which the petitioners reside, is situated on Buzzard's Bay, and in time of war exposed to the approach of the enemy in barges, which may be repulsed by well-disciplined infantry ; and that the standing Company in the village contains on its roll one hundred and ten men ; and praying to be authorized to raise by voluntary enlistment a Company of light infantry — ask leave to report : that the object of the petitioners appears to be approved by the Commanding officers of the regiment, brigade, and division, in which the petitioners reside ; and that it further appears that the facts set forth in said petition are true ; the Committee, therefore, for the reasons set forth in said petition, are of

---

* This is what came to be spoken of at New Bedford as the "OLD GUARDS," to distinguissh it from another company that succeeded it a few years later, and also called *New Bedford Guards*. The "Old Guards," were a large, elegantly uniformed, finely equipped and very excellently drilled company. Hon. H. G. O. Colby, was their first commander. Hon. Lincoln F. Brigham, succeeded him. The last company, had George A. Bourne, for their First Commander, and he was succeeded by Timothy Ingraham.

opinion that to grant the prayer thereof would conduce to the improvement of the militia, and in time of war add to the safety of said village. They therefore recommend that His Excellency, the Commander-in-Chief, be advised to issue his orders, authorizing the petitioners to raise by voluntary enlistment a Company of light infantry, to be annexed to the 4th Regiment of the 1st Brigade, 5th Division, and when organized to be recruited within the limits of the town of Rochester; provided, however, that before said Company shall be organized, not less than forty-five members be associated to form the same; and that the organization thereof shall be completed in six months from the first day of July next, and not afterwards. Which is respectfully submitted.

MARCUS MORTON, per order."

"In Council, June 18, 1825. — The within Report is accepted, and by the Governor approved.

EDWARD D. BANGS, Secretary."

"Commonwealth of Massachusetts; Head Quarters, Boston, June 21st, 1825. GENERAL ORDER. — The Commander-in-Chief, having approved the above written advice of Council, directs Major General Benj. Lincoln to carry the same into effect. By His Excellency's command,

WM. H. SUMNER, Adj't Gen'l."

" Head Quarters, New Bedford, July 5, 1825. DIVISION ORDERS. — Brigadier General Ward is charged with the execution of the foregoing advice of Council and General Order of the 21st ultimo.

By order of the Major General, Fifth Division,

TIMO. G. COFFIN, Aid-de-Camp.

" Head Quarters, Middleborough, Aug. 5th, 1825. BRIGADE ORDERS. — Lieut. Colo. Benja. Wood, Commandant of the 4th Regt., 1st Brig., 5th Div., is directed to carry into execution the foregoing order of Council, general order, and division order of the 5th of July, 1825, and to effect the complete organization of the Company alluded to in said order, as therein directed.

By order of the Brig. Gen'l, 1st Brigade, 5th Division.

NATHL. WILDER, Brigade Major."

This company of light infantry was raised, and Ebenezer Barrows elected and commissioned Captain of the same.

At the first choice of field officers for the 5th Regiment, Capt. Ebenezer Barrows was promoted to Lieut. Colonel.

The following gentlemen, residing within the limits of what is now Mattapoisett, held commissions in the local militia higher than that of captain:

Lieut. Col. Ebenezer Barrows, in 5th Regt., 1st Brigade, 5th Division, from 1826 to 1727.

Major Rogers L. Barstow, in 3d Regt. Light infantry, 2d Brigade, 1st Division Mass. volunteer Militia, from May, 1853, to 1858. Resigned and was honorably discharged.

TOWN OFFICERS, 1873-4.

Selectmen, Overseers of the Poor, and Assessors. — Franklin Cross, Wilson Barstow, Horace F. Shaw.

Town Clerk. — Thomas Nelson.

Treasurer and Collector. — Isaiah P. Atsatt.

School Committee. — Wm. Weaver, George Purinton, Jr., Weston Howland, Joshua L. Macomber, Joseph L. Cole.

Constables. — R. W. Bowles, Charles H. Nye.

Congregational Church (formerly First Parish, Rochester). Organized 27th July, 1736. Rev. Edward G. Smith, Pastor; Amittai B. Hammond, Noah Hammond, Deacons: Supt. Sabbath School, Samuel Sturtevant.

First Christian Church. — organized 1820 or thereabouts. Rev. Wm. Faunce, Pastor; Gideon B. Barlow, Deacon; Wm. R. Randall, Supt. Sabbath School.

Universalist Church. — Organized April 25, 1859; meeting house built several years previously. Have no settled Pastor for some years. Ivory Snow, Deacon.

Friends' Meeting — belonging to Long Plain Preparative Meeting, and to New Bedford Monthly Meeting.

Advent Chapel. — With no settled Pastor. Meetings held regularly.

MIDDLEBOROUGH.

In this brief sketch of one of the oldest, and until within a few years, superficially the largest town in the Commonwealth, it is not proposed to write all that can be or that ought to be written, all that it would be pleasant to tell, agreeable to hear, or profitable to treasure up in the memory, as we have neither the materials, the time or opportunity, to collect the necessary facts, or the space in this work to present the same in an intelligible and readable form.

One of the best men that our country ever produced, very truly remarked, "every particle of historic truth is precious," and to that conclusion of his, doubtless, we owe the knowledge of very many important facts in the early history of our country, that but for his appreciation of their value and importance, would have been suffered to pass into forgetfullness, and buried in oblivion.

No inconsiderable portion of this town's history, has already appeared in print, and may be found by reference to the reports of the Mass. Historical Society, the Bi-centennial address delivered in Oct. 1869, Barber's Historical Collections of Mass., Plymouth County Directory by Mr. Pratt, History of the different churches in Middleborough, and perhaps other publications of equal merit.

It is not to repeat what has been so well expressed, in these publications, or in any one of them, or to attempt the enumeration and description of those highly important events and occurrences that form the most enduring land marks in the towns history, but rather to gather up and present to our readers an account of circumstances and facts that have escaped the attention of most writers, but are nevertheless a part of the town's history, and are required to be known to enable any person to form correct conclusions concerning the whole.

As a part of Indian domain, Middleborough had been designated as "*Namasket*" and the tribe inhabiting the locality, were led by a sachem, called Tispaquin.

Over forty years intervened between the date of the first settlement of the white people at Plymouth, and the incorporation of Middleborough, and several years later, at the breaking out of King Phillip's War, or fifty-five years after Plymouth was settled, the white inhabitants of Middleborough were too few in numbers to offer successful resistance to the assaults of infuriated red men, but deeming discretion the better part of valor, retreated to Plymouth, leaving their possessions at the disposal of the savages.

ANCIENT HOUSE IN MIDDLEBOROUGH, TAKEN DOWN IN 1870.
A part of it is said to have stood 200 years.

Among those inhabitants then fleeing to Plymouth, was John Nelson, who for several years was elected to the office of Selectman of Middleborough.

Upon the conclusion of hostilities, John Nelson returned to Middleborough, and is believed to have continued there during the remainder of his life. What relation John Nelson was to the Thomas Nelson, who settled on Assawamset Neck is not known. The wife of John Nelson was Mrs. Lydia Barnaby, of Plymouth, widow of James Barnaby of that place, and a daughter of Robert Bartlett, who came a passenger in the ship *Ann* that arrived in 1623. Lydia was born June 8, 1647. Her mother was Mary Warren, daughter of Richard Warren, a passenger in the May Flower in 1620, and one of the eleven persons (in their company of forty) who were allowed the title of "*Mister*."

Of those brave men that imperiled their lives, in "King Philip's War," Middleborough was for many years the home of one of the most distinguished. John Raymond, a soldier in Captain Joseph Gardiner's company of Salem, is said to have been the first man who entered the gate of the Indian Fort in the Narragansett country on that bloody afternoon, and in the most sanguinary conflict New England had ever seen, (Sunday Dec. 19, 1675.) His Captain, Joseph Gardiner, fell dead soon after entering the fort, being shot through the head. During the "Witch delusion at Salem," the veteran soldier John Raymond fled for his life, from those he had thus defended, and for whose protection, he had exposed both life and limb, and in Middleborough, sought safety from fanatical persecution and insane madness. It is gratifying to think that in Middleborough, this brave man, ill treated and unappreciated patriot, found a "city of refuge," and haven of rest, that here

"The broken soldier was kindly bade to stay,"

that here during the evening of his days, with none to hurt, harm, molest, or make afraid, he could

"Weep o'er his wounds, and tales of honor done,"
Shoulder his crutch, and show how fields were won."

After coming to reside in Middleborough, John Raymond the Narragansett soldier, became a member of the Congregational Church here gathered, "a soldier in the army of the Lord," and here at his death had his burial, and here his grave remains till this day. The precise date of his admission to membership in the first Congregational Church in Middleborough was April 29, 1722, when he was said to have been in the seventy-fourth year of his age, and if so he must have been born in or about 1648. June 5, 1725, the noble old veteran went to an " inspection " by the great Searcher of all hearts, and passed in " grand review " before the God of Armies and " Lord of Hosts." Seventy and seven was the number of the years of his earthly pilgrimage, in which he was compelled to watch and fight and pray.

Isaac Peirce, another soldier in the " Narragansett Expedition" who helped to fill the quota required from the town of Duxbury, became an inhabitant of Middleborough, (that part now Lakeville), and died there February 28, 1732, in the 71st. year of his age.

He, in common with those who at setting out for the field of slaughter were mustered on Dedham Plain, received, and trusted in the promise, that if he " played the man, took the fort and drove the enemy out of the Narragansett country, should have a gratuity of land," endured the difficulties those brave men went through in storming that fort in the depth of winter, and the pinching wants they underwent in pursuing those Indians that escaped through a hideous wilderness and which became famously known as the " *Hungry March.*"

Although but seventeen years old, when this promise was made, the dangers shared and hardship endured, Isaac Peirce lived to attain the age of three score and ten years, to die and lie buried in his grave several months before it was fullfilled. Nearly sixty years of petitioning and anxious waiting was required, now that the dangers were over, to induce the government of Mass. to meet its obligation and voluntary proposition, redeem its sacred promise made to her brave defenders, who met and conquered those dangers and averted the impending ruin, that threatened speedily to come upon the country, when the promise was made.

History continually repeats, itself Massachusetts was influenced and acted *then* as Congress is acting *now* by defeating bills to allow bounty lands to loyal soldiers, in the late war, and with unblushing effrontery urging as an objection that so very large an amount of land, will be required to meet the demand, and thus Congress now, as the legislative body of Mass. did then, are waiting for the soldiers to die off and become to their view "*beautifully less*" in numbers. Notwithstanding the large numbers slain on the battle fields of the late rebellion, there is no disguising the fact that too many, far to many, lived to return home, a great many more than politicians ever wished to see, and who they impatiently endure. No other government, or people ever treated her soldiers so ungratefully or so meanly in comparison with its power to recognize and ability to reward.

The first church in Middleborough, was gathered Dec. 26, 1694, and Samuel Fuller ordained pastor. He died the next year, aged 66. He was greatly lamented. Rev. Thomas Palmer, was the next minister, and his habits were such as to bring scandal upon him, and he was deposed. In 1709, was ordained as their pastor, the Rev. Peter Thacher, who was faithful and successful in his ministry, for nearly 35 years. He was succeeded by Rev. Sylvanus Conant, ordained in 1745, and who died of small pox in 1777. Next in order came Rev. Joseph Barker. He was ordained in 1781, and for a time represented a district in the House of Representatives in Congress. Rev. Israel Putnam also preached to this people, for quite a long term of years.

The 2nd precinct formed in the southwest part of Middleborough, in 1719, fell within the limits of Lakeville, at the division of the town in 1853. For further notice, *See Lakeville.*

Another division in the original church took place in 1847, when was formed, at the village called the Four Corners, the "*Central Congregational Church.*"

A Baptist church was formed in that part called *Titicut*, in 1748, and Rev Isaac Backus the historian of the Baptist, ordained as pastor.

A second Baptist church was formed in 1757, and Rev. Ebenezer Hinds, the next year was ordained pastor. This at the division of the town fell within the limits of Lakeville.

A third Baptist church was constituted in the southeast part of the town of Middleborough, in 1761, and Rev. Ebenezer Jones, ordained as pastor. He was succeeded in the ministry at this place, by Rev. Asa Hunt, of Braintree, 1771, and Rev. Samuel Nelson, of Middleborough, in 1794. Reverend Samuel Nelson, was a son of William Nelson of Middleborough (now Lakeville), and a brother of Rev. William Nelson, of Norton, Rev. Ebenezer Nelson of South Reading, and an uncle of Rev. Ebenezer Nelson jr., of Lynn, Mass. Rev. Samuel Nelson was a grand son of Thomas Nelson, the, first or earliest member of the Calvinistic Baptist denomination at Middleborough.

A fourth Baptist church was formed in that part of Middleborough now Lakeville, and worshipped in a church edifice called the " Pond Meeting House,', Rev. Ebenezer Briggs was their pastor. This meeting-house was changed into a dwelling house and a grocery store, and a part made use of as a public hall, called "Sassamon Hall," in honor of the praying Indian slain near this spot by order of Metacom, or King Philip. This edifice was burned in 1870. It stood about seventy-four years.

The "Central Baptist Church" in Middleborough, was formed in 1828, and a handsome church edifice, given to them by Major Levi Peirce, who held the office of deacon of that church for twenty years. He also liberally endowed the church. Added to this there are now two Methodist churches in town, one near Fall Brook, so called, and the other, at Four Corners Village; and quite a body of Roman Catholics who hold religious services in Peirces Hall.

In the French and Indian War, 1758, Captain Benjamin Pratt, raised a company that he took to the battle field as a part of Colonel Thomas Doty's regiment.

Nearly all this company, if not indeed every member, resided in what was then Middleborough, and consisted of the following named persons: Benjamin Pratt, Captain; Silvester Richmond, and David Sears, Lieutenants; Nelson Finney. Ensign; Seth Tinkham, Lemuel Harlow, Silas Wood, and Abial Cole, Sergeants; Archippus Cole, Seth Billington, Jesse Snow, and John Miller, Corporals; Perez Tinkham, and Jacob Tinkham, Musicians; Jacob Allen, Jesse Bryant. Joseph Bent, Abner Barrows, Abner Barrows, jr., Isaac Bennett, John Bennett, Samuel Bennett, Benjamin Barrows, Abraham Barden, William Barlow, Eliakim Barlow, John Barker, Perez Cobb, Onesemus Campbell, Gideon Cobb, Gershom Cobb, William Cushman, Peter Crapo, Thomas Caswell, Jesse Curtis, Ezekiel Curtis, Consider Chase, Jabez Doggett, Simeon Doggett, Ebenezer Dunham, Adam David, Elkanah Elmes, John Elmes, John Ellis, John Eaton, Asa French, William Fuller. Simeon Fuller, Jedediah Holmes, John Harlow, Zurel Haskell, Jeremiah Jones, Jeremiah Jones jr., John Knowlton, James Littlejohn, Robert Mackfun, Thomas Miller, David Miller, Noah Morse, Johnathan Morse, Jacob Muxum, Isaac Nye, Thomas Peirce, Job Peirce, Paul Pratt, Francis Pomeroy, Samuel Pratt, Samuel Pratt jr., Henry Richmond, Nathan Richmond, Job Richmond, Moses Reding, Noah Raymond, Barnabas Samson, Jabez Samson, Jacob Samson, Obadiah Samson, John Samson, Crispus Shaw, Perez Shaw, Zebedee Shaw, Peleg Standish, Robert Seekell, Benjamin Streeter, private soldiers.

Of the march of that company, Sergeant Seth Tinkham in a diary that he kept, recorded: "Middleborough May 29, 1758, we met at Elijah Clapp's a little after sun rise, and drawed up our men into a body, and called the roll, and then marched to Major Howard's, in Bridgewater, seven miles. There went to dinner, and then we marched to Newcomb's, in Norton, and there overtook the cart that had our packs, there we staid all night, and laid up chambers."

"May the 30, we marched by sunrise to Lieut. Man's, in Wrentham, eleven miles, there went to dinner, and then we marched to Dr. Corbett's, in Bellingham, ten miles, went to supper. After supper, Mr. Hinds preached a sermon to us, there our cart overtook us, there we stayed."

"May the 31, we marched to Mr. Graves' in Mendon, three miles, and there went to breakfast, and from there, we marched to John Holland's, in Sutton, fifteen miles, there went to supper, there the cart overtook us.

June ye 1st, we staid at Holland's all day, because of ye rain, and Mr. Hinds preached to us in Holland's barn. June ye 2, we staid and settled our Billeting Roll, and paid off several Their Billeting money, in the afternoon we marched to Worcester 4 miles, and there slept. June ye 3, we mustered our men by eight o'clock, in the morning, and drew up into a line with the Regiment, called over our Roll, and then our Company marched off, then our Captain left us and went to Boston. I and Archippus Cole staid at Worcester until next morning."

These extracts from Sergeant Tinkham's diary serve to show how minute and particular he was in noting down his observations and knowledge of the occurrences ot that march, and his entry, made under date of June 11, 1758, will probably remind some soldiers of the late war of the rebellion, of their own experiences by "flood and field," and also the disregard paid to the Sabbath day, so common among all nations, when engaged in war. "June 11, Sunday we marched till about noon, Through mud and water, over hills and mountains, the worst way that ever was, and about 2 o'clock in the afternoon, Came up a thunder Shower, and wet us as wet as we could be we marched a Little Farther and Incampt and set our Centrys. John Bennett and Perez Cobb went back a mile to fetch a sick man Belonging to Captain Hodgers who was gone forward."

This company participated in the disastrous attempt to tske Ticonderoga July 6 and 8, and under date of July 8,

1758, Sergeant Tinkham says: "We marched with the Light Infantry, They went forward, Col. Doty Brought up the Rear, in Sight of the Fort, there we Drawed up 4 Deep the Light Infantry about ten Rods before us Expecting Every moment To be fired upon, in the mean time Col. Johnson with a party of Indians upon the west side of ye Lake marched up to the Top of a hill where he with his Indians fired upon the Fort, with the hideous yelling of the Indians, the worst noise I ever heard, and Drove a party of French into the Lake "about Eleven o'clock the Regulars marched up and all the Rhode Islanders and a little past 12 o'clock they began To Fire upon the French, at the Breastwork which was made of heaped Timbers and a Treanch around it very strong, which was built after we drove the advanced guard off, had we gone forward at our first Landing, we could have got the ground. The Regulars Drawed up before the Breastwork, and fought against it with Small arms 5 hours, the French would fire upon them with their Artillery, and with one field piece killed 18 grenadiers dead upon the Spott, the number of men Lost is not ascertained, but by all accounts we Lost 3000; Besides wounded; had Major Rogers had his Liberty, and done as he Intended we should have Drawed them out of their Breastwork, but Col. Bradstreet Come up with his Regiment, and Drove on and Lost allmost all his men, our Artillery Came up the Lake, allmost to us and then was ordered Back, I know not for what Reason, and towards night we was ordered back to the advanced guard, and got there about 9 o clock, we had nothing to eat, the allowance we had before we Set out from Lake George, was not Enough for one Day, and we got no more untill we got Back." Jabez Doggett was wounded."

"July 9, we was ordered to go on board our Boats and go back to Lake George, which we did, and Rowed all Day, without any thing to Eat, we got back about Sunset, but could Draw no allowance untill next day, and so had nothing To Eat that night."

Three companies of "*Minute Men*," and two of militia from Middleborough, promptly responded to the *first call* of our country, on the ever memorable 19th of April 1775. These companies were commanded by Captains Abial Peirce, Nathaniel Wood, Wm. Shaw, Amos Wade, and Isaac Wood. The greater part of Capt. Abial Peirce's company, as also some members of the other companies resided in that part of Middleborough now Lakeville. Captain Abial Peirce had been a

Captain in the French and Indian War, fifteen years before that of the American Revolution.

When soldiers were required for a Continental Army, Captain Abial Peirce of Middleborough, raised a company

NOTE TO PAGE 28.

Until Lakeville was detached and set off from Middleborough, in 1853, the latter town was said to have contained a greater number of acres than any other in the State of Massachusetts.

NOTE TO PAGE 28.

Col. Benjamin Church made use of that expression in the preface to his history of King Philip's War, published in 1715.

A great deal of interesting and valuable information concerning Middleborough, can be found by reference to the printed reports of the *Mass. Historical Society*, being communications of gentlemen who formerly resided here, but who long since started on that journey, from whose bourne no traveller returns.

NOTE TO PAGE 28.

The Indian name has of late years been applied to a manufacturing company, and the river has ever retained it.

NOTE TO PAGE 30.

Bridgewater although equally exposed as Middleborough, surrounded as they were by the savage foe, and "strongly advised and solicited to desert their dwellings, and repair down to the towns on the sea side," resolutely kept their ground, and successfully defended their settlement. On the 8th of May 1676, Tispaquin, from Middleborough, with about three hundred of his Indians, made an assault upon the town, and set fire to many houses, but as said the old chronicles, "the inhabitants issuing from their houses fell upon them, so resolutely that the enemy were repelled, and a heavy shower of rain falling at the same time, the fires were soon extinguished." The close proximity of Tispaquin and his tribe was perhaps one reason why Middleborough was abandoned, and Bridgewater having been settled earlier was probably stronger and better prepared to defend itself than Middleborough.

Mrs. Lydia Barnaby of Plymouth, who after the decease of her husband, James Barnaby, became the wife of John Nelson, of Middleborough, during her first marriage, had become the mother of James Barnaby, jr. James Barnaby, jr., married Joanna Harlow, daughter of Sergeant William Harlow of Plymouth. James Barnaby, jr., was born in or about 1670. He purchased a farm in Freetown, for thirteen hundred pounds, which farm now, after the lapse of one hundred and forty-eight years, is still owned by his lineal descendants. The will of James Barnaby, bore date of June 22, 1726, and he died July 5th, 1726. Joanna, his wife, was born March 24, 1669, and she died Sept. 4, 1725. Their only son, Captain Ambrose Barnaby, was born at Plymouth, in 1706, died in Freetown, April 18, 1775. He married Elizabeth Gardiner, of Swanzey.

NOTE TO PAGE 32.

No religious meetings were held in their meeting house for many years, and it was finally sold, and remodelled into a hall called, "*Sansamon Hall*," and a part converted into a grocery store, together with a tenement for a family. Accidentally took fire and was burned to the ground, in the early part of 1870. Had stood about 75 years.

MIDDLEBOROUGH. 37

for Colonel Dyke's Regiment, and was put on duty at or near Boston. Captain Nathaniel Wood also raised a company that became a part of Col Simeon Cary's Regiment on duty at Roxbury; of Captain Nathaniel Wood's Co. Job Peirce, a brother of Captain Abial. was a Lieutenant. Lieut. Job Peirce, was promoted to Captain May 9th, 1776, and not long after commanded a company of men in an expedition to Rhode Island, where they served in a Regiment commanded by Colonel Theophilus Cotton, of Plymouth.

Captain Nathaniel Wood's Company of Militia that responded to the call of April 19th, 1775, entered on Rolls as 1st Company of Militia, of Middleborough.

Commissioned Officers. Nathaniel Wood, Captain; Amos Washburn, Lieutenant; Joseph Smith, 2d Lieutenant; Non Commissioned Officers. Zebadee Sprout, Jesse Vaughn, Ebenezer Thomas, Barney Cobb. Sergeants; John Pickens, Amos Wood, Joseph Ellis, Solomon Dunham, Corporals; Zebadee Pratt, Drummer; William Clapp, Fifer; Caleb Thompson, William Bennett, Nathan Wood, Seth Miller, Ephraim Thomas, Jr., William Armstrong, Isaac Bryant, Israel Rickard, Elisha Cox, William Raymond, Joseph Redding, John Darling, Ebenezer Smith, James Thomas, Perez Thomas, Andrew Cushman, Micha Leach, William Wood, David Shaw, John Hackett, Zurashada Palmer, George Richmond, George Leonard, Elezer Thomas, Jr., Samuel Pickens, Jr., Joseph Vaughan, Jr., Benjamin Leonard, Nathan Leonard, Jacob Miller, Nathaniel Thompson, Jonathan Samson, Jonathan Ryder, Samuel Raymond, Soloman Thomas, Seth Peirce, Caleb Tinkham, Jos. Richmond, Jr., Samuel Rickard, David Vaughn, Edmund Wood, Privates.

Captain William Shaw's company called on the rolls 1st company of "*Minute Men*" from Middleborough, April 19th, 1775.*

Commissioned Officers. William Shaw, Captain; Joshua Benson, Jr., Lieutenant; William Thompson, 2d Lieutenant; Non Commissioned Officers. David Thomas, Ebenezer Cobb, 2d, James Smith, Caleb Bryant, Sergeants; Job Randall, John Soule, Peter Bates, James Cobb, Corporals; Sylvanus Raymond, Drummer; Samuel Torry, Fifer; Elisha Thomas, Nelson Finney, Lemuel Harlow, Isaac Thompson,

* The first attempt to prepare for defence was by organizing military companies, each member of which pledged himself to be in readiness to march at a moment's notice, and hencethe ssame came to be called "MINUTE MEN." After Lexington fight, these were succeeded by companies enlisted for a term of months or years.

Edmund Wood, Jr., Zenas Cushman, Joseph Pratt. Phineas Thomas, Caleb Thompson Jr., Elisha Paddock. Nathan Bennett, John Soule, 2d, Gideon Cobb, Eliakim Barlow, Ephraim Cushman, Barnabas Cushman, Ichabod Benson, Ebenezer Raymond, Solomon Raymond, Thomas Bates, Asa Benson, Samuel Raymond, 2d, Elipha' Thomas, Silvas' Bennett, 3d, Joseph Thomas, William Le Barron, John Perkins, Joseph Shaw, Joshua Eddy, Seth Eddy, Jos' Chamberlain, Ebenezer Bennett, Ebenezer Briggs, 3d, Asa Barrows, Benjamin Barden, Jacob Thomas, Nathan Darling, John Sampson, Thomas Shaw, Japeth Le Baron, Abiezer Le Barron, Joseph Bennett. Private Soldiers.

Captain Amos Wade's company of "*Minute Men*" from Middleborough, April 19th 1775, called on rolls, third company of Minute Men.

Commissioned Officers. Amos Wade, Captain; Archipus Cole, Lieutenant; Lemuel Wood, Ensign; Non Commissioned Officers. Isaac Perkins, Ichabod Churchill, Isaac Shaw, Joseph Tupper, Sergeants; Isaiah Keith, Lot Eaton, Corporals; John Shaw, Drummer; Daniel White, Fifer; Zebulon Vaughn, Abner Pratt, Nathan Pratt, Joseph Leonard 5th, Elnathan Wood, Joseph Hathaway. Michael Leonard, David Weston, Samuel Pratt, William Fuller, James Keith, Silas Leonard, Stephen Robinson, Daniel Hills, Stephen Richmond, Lazarus Hathaway, Peter Tinkham, Thomas Harlow, John Drake, Levi Hathaway, Moses Leonard, Solomon Howard, Nathaniel Richmond, Jonathan Washburn, Thomas Cobb, Edmund Richmond, Seth Richmond, Asa Richmond, Joseph Leonard 3d, Solomon Beals, Jonathan Richmond, Zepheniah Shaw, Elijah Alden, Joseph Clark, Benjamin Hafford, Privates.

Captain Isaac Wood's company of "*Minute Men*" that marched from Middleborough April 19th, 1775, called on rolls 2d company of minute men.

Commissioned Officers. Isaac Wood, Captain; Corneilus Tinkham, Lieutenant; Abram Townsend, Ensign; Non Com missioned Officers. Abner Bourne, Joseph Holmes, John Benson, William Harlow, Sergeants; Samuel Wood, Foxel Thomas, Abner Nelson, Joseph Churchill, Corporals; Peregaine White, Drummer; Seth Fuller, Fifer; Robert Sprout, George Samson, Josiah Harlow, Gershom Foster, Ebenezer Elms, Consider Barden, Consider Fuller, John Barrows, John Townsend Jr., Gideon Southworth, John Smith 3d, Samuel Wood Jr., Elisha Clark, Abraham Parris, Noah

Holmes 2d, Ebenezer Barrows Jr., Elisha Peirce, Abisha Samson, Samuel Barrows, Peter Miller, George Thomas, Thomas Wood 2d, Eb. Howland, Moses Samson, Daniel Tinkham, Elisha Rider, Isaac Cushman, Abraham Shaw, Samuel Muxum, James Shaw, Samuel Ransom, James Peirce Job Smith, Seth Samson, Levi Peirce, George Williamson, Abial Chase, John Tinkham Jr., Nat Holmes 3d, Peleg Hathaway, Peter Hoar, Andrew Cole, Aaron Cary, Bartlett Handy, Arodi Peirce, John Holloway, James Ashley, Levi Jones, Jotham Caswell, William Read 3d, Ephraim Reynolds, Jonathan Hall, Joseph Hathaway, Samuel Parris, Ebenezer Hinds, Philip Hathaway, Isaac Hathaway, John Townsend, Henry Peirce, Privates.

Captain Peter H. Peirce, son of Capt. Job. Peirce, and Captain Greenleaf Pratt, each commanded a company, of the coast guard raised in Middleborough, and put on duty in or near Plymouth, in 1814.

Major Levi Peirce, a son of Captain Job Peirce, was detailed, and served as a Major of the coast guard stationed at New Bedford and Fairhaven, in the last war with England.

The militia of Middleborough, from the date of incorporation until about 1720, was embraced in one company. Then it was divided into two, known as first and second companies, and about twenty years later, divided into three companies, and ere long into four, and thus continued until the war of the revolution, when again subdivided, and organized as seven companies. That part of the town of Middleborough now Lakeville, embraced all the 7th company, nearly or quite all the 4th, and a part of the 2d. Increase in population caused another division, so that at one time Middleborough had nine companies of local militia. Some of these were disbanded at the raising of two grenadier companies, in the town in 1818.

There existed in Middleborough for many years, two grendier companies known generally as "*Middleborough Guards,*" and "*Old Colony Guards,*" the first named being raised from those members of the "train band" residing at and near the Four Corners village, and the other from those living near Fall Brook, and for which circumstance the last named company came to be called "*Fall Brook Co.*" The Middleborough Guards were organized pursuant to orders of which the following is a true copy.

"Commonwealth of Massachusetts."
In Council January 20th, 1818.

The military committee to whom was referred the petition of Thomas Wood, and forty-three others, privates in a company of militia in the town of Middleborough, commanded by Captain Enoch Haskins, praying, that said company may be disbanded and. annexed to the company commanded by Captain Sylvanus Warren, in order from the united companies, to enlist and form a Grenadier company, observe that the Colonel and Lieutenant Colonel of the Regiment of which said companies are a part, being the 4th Regiment in the first Brigade of the fifth Division of the Militia, approve of the object of the petitions, and state that the Captain of the company to which they belong, has no objections to the proposed measure and that the Lieutenant has removed out of the bounds of the Brigade, while the Ensign explicitly gives his assent, and the committee further observe that the measure prayed for, meets the approbation of the Brigadier and Major Generals—report that His Excellency be advised to direct that the company first above mentioned, be disbanded, and that the non-commissioned officers and privates thereof, be annexed to the company, now commanded by Captain Sylvanus Warren, the limits of which shall be extended so as in future to comprehend the district of the disbanded company and to authorize Sylvanus Barrows, named for the purpose in said petition, to enlist from the said united companies a proper number of men, to form a company of Grenadiers which shall be annexed to the fourth Regiment aforesaid."

"D. Cobb, per order."

"In Council, January 22d, 1818. This report is accepted, and by the Governor approved."

"A. Bradford, Secretary of the Commonwealth."

"Commonwealth of Massachusetts,"
"General Order,"
"Head Quarters, Boston, February 25th 1818."

"The Commander in Chief having approved the above written advice of Council, directs the same to be carried into effect. Major General Nathaniel Goodwin will give the necessary orders for that purpose."

"By His Excellency's command,
Fitch Hall, Acting Adjutant General."

"Head Quarters, Plymouth, March 7th 1818."
Division Orders.

The Major General directs Brigadier General Washburn, to issue the necessary orders for forming a company of Grenadiers, in the 4th Regiment, agreeable to advice of Council and General Orders of the 25th ultimo.

By order of Major General, 5th Division,
N. Hayward, A. D. C., to Major General.

" Head Quarters, Middleborough, March 11th 1818."
Brigade Orders.

The Brigadier General directs Colonel Ephraim Ward, to issue the necessary orders for forming and organizing a company of Grenadiers in the 4th Regiment. " agreeable to above General and Division orders"

" By order B. General, 1st Brigade,
Nathaniel Wilder Jr., B. Major."

The company was organized by the choice of Isaac Stevens, Captain. Lorenzo Wood, Lieutenant, and Sylvanus Barrows, Ensign. Stevens was Ensign of Captain Enoch Haskin's company, at the date of its disbandment.

The commanders or captains of this Grenadier company, were as follows:

Isaac Stevens from April 3d, 1818 to —— 1823.
Sylvanus Barrows from Sept. 9th 1823 to —— 1827.
Job Peirce, from April 24th 1827 to April 25th 1829.
Rufus Alden, from June 8th 1829 to —— 1830.
Josiah Tinkham, from April 28th, 1830, to 1833.
Abial P. Wood, May 7th, 1833. to 1835.
Morton Freeman, from April 2d, 1835, to 1840.
Jacob T. Barrows, from 1840 to 1842.
Amasa T. Thompson, from May 12 1842 to 1844.
Daniel Atwood, from ——1844 to July 10th 1844.
Andrew J. Pickens, from Aug. 3d, 1844, to 1846.
Dexter Phillips, from March 20th, 1846, to 1847.
Arad Bryant, from February 20th, 1847, to 1849.
Albert Thomas, from May 20th, 1849, to 1851.
Joseph Sampson Jr., from 1851 to Nov. 28, 1851, the date of its disbandment.

The company disbanded by act of the Governor and Council, January 20th 1818, was what was known as the " Second company" in the local militia of Middleborough, and had existed nearly one hundred years. It was formed as nearly as can now be ascertained, in 1720, and Nathaniel Smith commissioned as its first Captain.

The bounds of this Second company extended into what is now Lakeville, to the brook that crosses the road in said town a little beyond the present residence of John H. Nelson.

The name of those gentlemen who successively held the office of Captain of the Second company, together with the dates of their commissions, as far as said dates are now within our knowledge, were as follows:

Nathaniel Smith, 1720.
Gideon Southworth.
Nathaniel Smith, Jr.
John Barrows.
Robert Sprout.
Abial Peirce, from April, 1775 to 1775.
Abner Bourne, from June 2d 1780 to July 1, 1781.
George Vaughan, from April 20, 1790 to ——— 1793.
Peter Hoar, from June 5th, 1793, to January 4th, 1797.
Jabez Thomas, from Jan. 25, 1797, to 1799
John Morton, from May 7, 1799, to 1802.
Sylvanus Tillson, from May 11, 1802, to 1805.
Nathaniel Cole, from May 7, 1805 to 1811.
Ephraim Ward, from March 18, 1811, to October, 1813.
Peter H. Pierce, from February 18, 1814, to ——— 1816.
Orrin Tinkham, from Sept. 10, 1816, to 1817.
Enoch Haskins, from ——— 1817, to January 20th, 1818, the date of disbandment by order of Governor and Council.

The Second Grenadier company in the town of Middleborough, that known as "the Old Colony Guards," or "Fall Brook Company," was raised and organized according to the following orders.

"In Council, May 11th, 1818. The military committee of Council, to whom was referred the petition of Roland Peirce, and other inhabitants of the town of Middleborough, requesting that the Military Company in said town, commanded by Captain Nathaniel Hall, may be disbanded, the officers of said company approving the measure, and the non-commissioned officers and privates of the same be annexed to the company now commanded by Capt. Pelham Atwood, and that said Peirce, and his associates may be permitted to form themselves into a Grenadier company, repectfully report that His Excellency be advised to have the company of militia in the town of Middleborough, commanded by Captain Nathaniel Hall, in the fourth Regiment, first Brigade and fifth Division, disbanded and the non-commissioned officers and privates of the same annexed to the adjoining company now commanded by Captain Pelham Atwood and to direct that the limits heretofore of said Hall's company shall hereafter be considered as forming a part of the aforesaid Captain Atwood's company, and likewise to permit the aforesaid Roland Peirce, and his associates under the enlistment of Captain Nathaniel Hall, to form themselves into a company of Grenadiers together with such others as may hereafter join them from within the limits of said town of Middleborough, and when organized to have them annexed to the aforesaid fourth Regiment, provided however that none of the standing companies of Middleborough, are thereby reduced to a less number than is required by law.

"D. Cobb, per order."

Then followed from the Adjutant General, an order dated May 11th 1818, and from Major General Nathaniel Goodwin of Plymouth, a Division order of May 19th 1818, and Brigadier General Abiel Washburn's Brigade order of May 23d 1818, the last directed to Colonel Ephraim Ward of the 4th Regiment, and the company was organized by the choice of Jonathan Cobb, Captain; Loring Miller, Lieutenant; and Darius Miller, Ensign. The Captains of this Grenadier company, with dates of commissions, were as follows:

Jonathan Cobb, from July 16, 1818, to —— 1824.
Darius Miller, from May 19, 1824 to September 12, 1828.
Lothrop S. Thomas, from April 21, 1830, to —— 1834.
Levi Morse, from Sept. 27th, 1834, to 1837.
Sylvester F. Cobb, from Sept. 20, 1837, to 1842.
Ichabod F. Atwood, from July 26, 1842, to 1847.
George Ward, from —— 1847, to May, 1850.
Stephen Thomas, from May 29, 1850, to April 3, 1852.
Lothrop Thomas, from May, 1852, to ——18—.
Thomas Weston, from 185– to 1856.
Robert M. Thomas, from —— 1856, to —— 1857.
Sylvanus Barrows, from 1857 to 1857, the date of its disbandment.

During the time that Ephraim Ward of Middleborough, (now Lakeville), held the office of Brigadier General, the first Brigade of fifth Division, then embracing all the militia of Plymouth County, paraded and mustered twice as a Brigade, and at other times mustered by Regiment. Both musters by Brigade were in the town of Halifax. The first on the farm of Thomas Drew, Esq., on Thursday the 20th day of September, 1826, and the other on the farm of Isaac Thompson, Thursday October 9th 1828. The Brigade consisted of five Regiments of Infantry, a Battalion of Artillery, and a Squadron of Cavalry, at the first muster, and the same at last save that the Cavalry had been reduced to one company, commanded by Captain Ira Clark, of Rochester, and some part of which generally belonged in Middleborough.

44   HISTORY OF TOWNS IN PLYMOUTH COUNTY.

This company, with another of like arm in Bridgewater, were made a Battalion of Cavalry, commanded by a Major. The first captain of this company was Hushia Thomas of Middleborough. William Bourne of Middleborough, who was commissioned as captain of this company of cavalry May 22, 1797, was promoted to Major of the Battallion, Sept. 12, 1803, and held that office until 1807.

Seth Southworth, and Nehemiah Leonard, of Middleborough, were captains at later dates and Harry Jackson of Middleborough now Lakeville, was Major. The local or standing companies of militia in Middleborough, to the commencement of the Revolutionary War, were a part of the first regiment, but at that date these, with the militia of Rochester, and Wareham, were detached and made to constitute a regiment known as the " Fourth Regiment," * and of which the following named Middleborough gentlemen, held the office of Colonel. Ebenezer Sprout, from 1775 to 1781, John Nelson from July 1, 1781 to 1787, Edward Sparrow, from 1794 to 1796, Abial Washburn, from July 22, 1800, to Sept. 4, 1816, Ephraim Ward, from 1817 to Jan. 27, 1825, Benjamin P. Wood, from 1826 to 1829, Darius Miller, from 1829 to 1831, Thomas Weston jr., from 1831 to 1834, Edward G. Perkins, from 1837 to 1839, Nathan King, from 1839 to April 24, 1840.

Names of Lieut. Colonels of the 4th regiment residing in Middleborough : William Tupper, from July 1st, 1781, to 1785 ; Edward Sparrow, from 1787, to 1794 ; Abial Washburn, from Jan. 4, 1797, to July 22, 1800 ; Peter Hoar, from July 22, 1800, to 1806 ; Jacob Cushman, from 1807 to 1809 ; Levi Peirce from 1812 to 1816 ; Ephraim Ward, from 1816, to April 25, 1817 ; Peter Hoar Peirce, from April 25, 1817 ; Benjamin P. Wood, from 1823 to Sept. 4, 1826 ; Southworth Ellis, from Sept. 4, 1826, to 1829 ; Thomas Weston, Jr., from Aug. 31, 1829, to 1832 ; Oliver Eaton, from 1832 to 1834 ; Edward G. Perkins, from 1834 to 1837 ; Nathan King, from 1837 to 1839.

Names of Middleborough gentlemen, who held the commission of a Brigadier General : Abial Washburn, from Sept. 4, 1816 to Dec. 1824, Ephraim Ward, from Jan. 27, 1825

---

* Before being Colonel of the new Fourth Regiment, Ebenezer Sprout had held the commission of Major in the First Regiment.

The first field officers of Fourth Regiment, were Ebenezer Sprout of Middleborough, Colonel ; Ebenezer White of Rochester, Lieut. Colonel ; Israel Fearing of Wareham, First Major ; John Nelson, of Middleborough, now Lakeville, Second Major.

to 1828, Darius Miller, from 1831 to 1833, Eliab Ward, from April 1850 to Oct. 1855.

The following named gentleman of this town held the commission of Field Officers, of the Third Regiment of Light Infantry.

Colonels, Eliab Ward, from July 10, 1844 to April, 1850; Elnathan W. Wilbur, from May 1850, to Jan. 1853; Stephen Thomas, from March, 1853 to 1858.

Lieutenant Colonel. Lothrop S. Thomas, from 1834 to 1836; Eliab Ward, from 1843 to July 10, 1844; Daniel Atwood, 1845 to 1850; Ebenezer W Peirce, April 3, 1852, to Nov. 7, 1855; Thomas Weston, 1856 to 1858.

Majors. Daniel Atwood, from July 10, 1844, to 1845; Joseph Sampson, jr., from 1845 to 1849; Elnathan W. Wilbur, from 1849 to May, 1850; George Ward, from May 1850, to 1851; Ebenezer W. Peirce, from Aug. 2, 1851, to April 3, 1852; Stephen Thomas, April 3, 1852, to March, 1853.

Squadron of Cavalry. Wm. Bourne, Major.

Battallion of Artillery. William Thomas, Major from 1834 to 1836.

Two companies of the Third Regiment, Light Infantry belonged in Middleborough. The other companies were from Halifax, Plymouth, Hanson, Abington, Plympton. William Thomas, of Middleborough, as Major of the Plymouth County Battallion of Artillery, was promoted from the office of Captain of Hanover Artillery Company.

July 1st 1781, John Nelson was promoted to Colonel, William Tupper, Lieut. Colonel, and Edward Sparrow, Major. They were all of Middleborough.

Colonel John Nelson lived in that part of Middleborough, now Lakeville. His former residence is now the home of Lieut. James Sampson, his great grand son, who did good service in the Union Army in late war of Rebellion. He resigned the offices of town clerk and town treasurer of Lakeville, to take a place in that army.

Colonel Edward Sparrow resided in that part of Middleborough called Fall Brook. General Abial Washburn was a son of Edward Washburn, of that part of the town now Lakeville. Abial Washburn received the appointment of Adjutant, when the Regiment was commanded by Colonel. (afterward General), Isreal Fearing of Wareham, and dated Oct. 2d, 1788; promoted to Major, May 1, 1794, Lieut. Col. Jan. 4, 1797, Colonel July 22, 1800, Brigadier General, Sept. 4, 1816. Honorably discharged in 1824.

Colonel (afterward Gen.) Ephraim Ward was a native of Carver.

Colonel Benjamin P. Wood came from the State of Vermont.

Ebenezer W. Peirce Encampment, Grand Army of the Republic, Post 8, of Mass. has its Head Quarters at the Four Corners Village, in Middleborough, Job Morton Staples, of Lakeville, Commander. Charles L. Starkey, Senior Vice Commander. Lyman Mason, jr., Junior Vice Commander. H. E. W. Petiy, Adjutant. Frederick Wood, Quartermaster. Simeon Harlow, Surgeon. Luther Crane, Chaplain. Benjamin W. Bump, Officer of the Day. Cyrus M. Vaughn, Quarter Master's Sergeant.

Job Morton Staples, commander of Ebenezer W. Peirce Encampment was a soldier in the Second Regiment Mass. Cavalry, in the late war of Rebellion, and a great grand son of Captain Henry Peirce, soldier in the French and Indian wars, and a captain in the patriot army of the Revolution.

Justices of the Peace, with dates of appointment.

Peter Oliver, 1748; John Fearing, 1755; Ebenezer Sprout, August 28th, 1775; Joshua White, August 28th, 1775; Samuel Clark, April 7th, 1787; Isaac Thompson, April 26th, 1787; James Sprout, July 5th, 1789; John Nelson, July 18th, 1791; Nehemiah Bennett, February 20, 1795; Wilks Wood, March 2d, 1800; David Richmond, May 24th, 1800; James Washburn, February 20th, 1804; Samuel Pickens, January 23d, 1808; John Tinkham, February 20th, 1808; William Thompson, March 5th, 1808; Zachariah Eddy, February 17th, 1810; Martin Keith, September 3d, 1810; Peter Hoar, February 5th, 1811; Thomas Weston, February 22d, 1811; Seth Miller Jr., November 14th, 1811; Hercules Cushman, October 29, 1811; Calvin Pratt, January 25th, 1812; William Canedy, August 3d, 1812; Jacob Bennett, June 9th, 1813; Cyrus Keith, June 9th, 1813; Thomas Sturtevant, June 9th, 1813; Abial Washburn, October 29th, 1814; William Bourne, February 16th, 1816; Charles Hooper, June 10th, 1817; Noah Clark, February 3d, 1818; Joshua Eddy Jr., January 23th, 1819; Levi Peirce, June 19th, 1819; Amos Washburn, September 7th, 1821; Thomas Bennett, November 21st, 1821; Ebenezer Pickens, January 16th, 1822; Isaac Stevens, January 23d, 1822; Abner Clark, January 10th, 1823; Abial P. Boothe, August 26th, 1823; William Nelson, February 17, 1824; Oliver Peirce, February 17th, 1824; Peter H. Peirce, July 1st, 1825; Samuel Thompson February 15th, 1826;

Ebenezer W. Peirce.

Seth Ewton, January 2d, 1828 ; Paul Hathaway, June 11th, 1829 ; Arad Thompson, June 9th, 1830 ; Reeland Tinkham, June 16th, 1831 ; Joshua Hoskins Jr., April 24th, 1832 ; Benjamin P. Wood, March 26th, 1833 ; Bradford Harlow. March 26th, 1833 ; Luther Washburn, August 25th, 1835 ; Jonathan Cobb, March 18th, 1836 ; Abizer T. Harvey, Janurry 27th, 1837 ; Silas Pickens, March 15th, 1837 ; Eliab Ward, March 6th, 1838 ; Abisha T. Clark, August 24th, 1841 ; Corneilus B. Wood, March 31st, 1842 ; Bela Kingman, December 17th, 1842 ; Nathan King, January 5th, 1843 ; Gamaliel Rounsevill, March 14th, 1843 ; George Sturtevant, March 14th, 1843 ; Stillman Benson, March 14th, 1843 ; Tisdale Leonard, September 20th, 1843 ; Andrew Weston, October 31st, 1843 ; William H. Wood, February 3d, 1844 ; James G. Thompson, July 1st, 1845 ; Apollos Hoskins, March 31st, 1846 ; Everett Robinson, July 7th, 1848 ; Philander Washburn, June 5th, 1849 ; Ichabod F. Atwood, October 2d, 1849 ; Zebulon Pratt, April 25th, 1850 ; Joshua Wood, March 12th, 1851 ; Asa T. Winslow, March 19th, 1851 ; George W. Wood, May 7th, 1851 ; Alfred Wood Jr., February 8th, 1854 ; Josiah Richards, March 15th, 1854.

Coroners. Nathaniel Foster Jr., March 4th 1782 ; Mark Haskell. February 22d, 1799 ; Dean Briggs, January 23d, 1808 ; Joseph Clark Jr., June 16th, 1809 ; Levi Briggs, February 16th, 1811 ; Peter H Peirce, February 16th, 1811 ; Asa Barrows, January 25th, 1812 ; Abiatha Briggs, May 15th, 1812 ; Joseph Jackson, May 4th, 1819 ; Ebenezer Strobridge, February 11th, 1820.

TOWN OFFICERS, 1873-4.

Selectmen, and Assessors.—Joseph T. Wood, Lewis Leonard, Stillman Benson.

Town Clerk, Treasurer and Collector. — C. B. Wood.

School Committee. — Henry L. Edwards, Augustus H. Soule, Hannah Crossman.

CHURCHES.

First Congregational Church. — Rev. E. N. Hidden, Pastor.
Central Congregational Church. — Rev. E. R. Drake, Pastor.

Baptist Church. — Rev. G. F. Fairbanks, Pastor.
Baptist Church. — Rev. Joseph J. Hutchinson, Pastor.
Methodist Church. — Rev. S. J. Carroll, Pastor.
Methodist Church. — South Middleborough, Rev. Mr. Sayre, Pastor.
Baptist Church. — Rock Middleborough, Rev. I. J. Burgess, Pastor.

SOCIETIES.

Assawampsett Division, S. of T. No. 34.

A. B. Bosworth, W. P.; Mary Miner, W. A; J. E. Beals, R. S; J. P. McCulley, F. S; Hattie Barden, Treasurer; Henry C. Richardson, Con. Meets Monday Evenings, at Soule's Hall.

Masonic. May Flower Lodge, Middleborough.

Officers. Charles N. Carpenter, Master. Roland F. Barrows, Sen. Warden. Frank R. Eaton, Jun. Warden. Chas. E. Leonard, Treasurer. James M. Coombs, Secretary. B. F. Tripp, Sen. Deacon. F. A. Sherman, Jun. Deacon. Charles L. Starky, Sen. Steward. James F. Roberts, Jun. Steward. S. Loring, Tyler. Meetings first Tuesday evening each month.

PEMBROKE.

A part of Duxbury was set off in 1711, incorporated as a new and distinct town and called Pembroke. First and foremost in those early times in old Colony history, on incorporating a new town, was the act of providing for the settlement of a gospel minister, and Pembroke did not form an exception to that Puritanic rule, as Rev. Daniel Lewis, was in 1712, ordained for that work, and there continued in the pastoral office for about thirty-nine years. He was succeeded by Rev. Thomas Smith, who ministered to the people for thirty-four years. Thus we see that two ministers supplied the pulpit of Pembroke for seventy-three years.

Next came Rev. Mr. Whitman, who continued in the ministry about nine years, and then a young man who had been a Missionary to the Indians at Marshpee, and died after preaching here a little more than one year. Rev. Morrill Allen, a graduate of Brown University, was settled here in 1801.

The first saw mill erected in Plymouth Colony is said to have been within the limits of what is now Pembroke.

The first entry of any kind made upon the town records of Pembroke, was that of a vote to pay John Peirce for sweeping the meeting house.

Company of "Minute Men" from the West Parish of Pembroke, that part now Hanson, that reponded to the country's first call, April 19th, 1775.

Commissioned Officers. Elijah Cushing, Captain ; Edward Thomas, Lieutenant ; Lemuel Barney, 2d Lieutenant : Non-Commissioned Officers. Joshua Barker, Simeon Jones, Noah Bonney, Snow Baker, Sergeants. Isaac Hobart, Drummer. Jacob Hatch, Fifer. Henry Perry, William Phillips jr., Richard Phillips, Gideon Ramsdell jr., Jacob Leavett, Abel Bourne, Mathew Fillage, Samuel Hill, Alexander Soper jr., Benjamin Ramsdell jr., Elisha Records, Samuel Bonney, Edward Heyford, Joseph Hollis, Adam Perry, Gamaliel Bosby, Noah Perry, Howland Beals, Joseph Bonney, Nathaniel Cushing, Elijah Cushing jr., Henry Munro jr., Thomas Osborn, John Bonney, George Osborn jr., Levi Wade, Abraham Jocelyn, Nehemiah Ramsdell, Isiah Bearce. Isaac Thomas, Jacob Bearse, Ichabod Howland, Mathew Whitten jr., John Whitten, Joseph Howland, James Torrey, Thomas Record, Ebenezer Bonney, Samuel Ramsdell jr., Josiah Cushing jr., Lot Dwelly, Richard Baker, Richard Lowden, Reuben Harden, George Osborn, James Tilson, Seth Bearce, Francis Josselyn, Joshua Pratt, Gain Robertson, Gain Robertson jr., John Jeffery, Theodore Cushing, Private Soldiers.

PEMBROKE TOWN OFFICERS, 1873-4.

Town Clerk — George H. Ryder.

Selectmen, Assessors, and Surveyors of Highways, and Overseers of the Poor — W. H. H. Bryant, Julius Cushman, Hervey Dyer.

Treasurer — Seth Whitman.

Collector — Francis Collamore.

School Committee — Nathan T. Shephard, Edward G. Barnard, Elias C. Scott.

Constables — Theodore S. Chandler, Francis Collamore, Benjamin T. Gardner.

CHURCHES.

Unitarian Church — Rev. Theophilus P. Daggett, Pastor.

Methodist Episcopal Church — Rev. J. W. Malcolm, Pastor.

Friends' Society — Church at North Pembroke.

G. A. R. — Post George A. Simmons, Meet, at Mechanics' Hall.

Indian Head Division, No. 48, S. of T. — Meets at Mattakeesett Hall.

Pembroke Total Abstinence Society.

President, Francis Collamore. Secretary, George H. Ryder. Treasurer, Seth Whitman.

PLYMPTON.

Plympton occupies the most central position of any township in the county, and its limits were formerly those of a religious parish in Plymouth, set off and incorporated as a town, in 1707, or about one hundred and sixty-six years ago. The early congregational ministers were Rev. Isaac Cushman, Rev. Jonathan Parker, Rev. Ezra Sampson, Rev. Eben Withington, Rev. John Briggs, and Rev. Elijah Dexter, the last named of whom was ordained in 1809, or one hundred and two years after the incorporation of the town, and thus it appears that five ministers supplied the pulpit for an entire century, or on an average twenty years each.

But of this time, Rev. Jonathan Parker appears to have performed a ministry of about fiorty-five years, as he was ordained to that work in 1731, and died in 1776, no other person appearing to have been employed in that office by this town during that period, nor until ten years afterward (unless temporarily) when he was succeeded by Rev. Mr. Sampson in 1786. Plympton was for several years the home of Deacon Lewis Bradford, quite distinguished as an antiquarian, and for his historical researches pertaining to this and other old Colony towns. Deacon Bradford was town clerk of Plympton and Representative to the General Court at Boston. A company of riflemen were raised in this town about 38 years since, and Abial Washburn commissioned Captian. The uniform consisted of green frock coats, and white pantaloons, and military caps, and plumes. Captain Washburn remained in command about eight years, and was succeeded by Erastus Leach as Captain, and the uniform was then changed to green dress coats, with red trimmings, black pantaloons with red stripe, and black bell topped caps. Captain James Ellis was the next Captain.

This company was changed to Infantry and made a part of the Third Regiment in Second Brigade of First Division Mass. Volunteer Militia, and as such responded to the *first call* for soldiers in the late war of the great rebellion, and performed a tour of three months' service at and near Fortress Munroe, in Virginia, as a part of Colonel David W. Wardrop's regiment and in the Brigade commanded by Brigdier General Ebenezer W. Peirce of Freetown.

When made an Infantry company, the uniform was changed to blue frock coats and blue pantaloons with white trimmings.

Under the former order that existed in the militia, viz., when the "*train bands,*" and "*alarm lists*" of Plymouth County, constituted a Brigade of four or five regiments of infantry with a squadron of Cavalry, and a Battalion of Artillery. Plympton was not unfrequently the scene of military operations, such as company trainings, regimental musters, military elections, and courts martial.

These in that quiet town have now so completely gone out of sight, been so thoroughly discontinued, as to the view of a casnal observer to leave no trace of their former prominence, or even existence, and yet the postive proof is still extant that such was the fact.

As our authorities, we will now give copies of orders from Major General Nathaniel Goodwin, of Plymouth, then commanding the Fifth Division of the militia of Mass., which division comprised the "*train bands*" and "*alarm lists*" of the counties of Barnstable, Bristol and Plymouth.

General Goodwin was a veteran officer of the patriot army in the war of the revolution, and is thought to have been the person referred to in that familiar stanza of Yankee Doodle.

"Father and I went down to camp,
Along with Captain Goodwin;
And there we see the boys and gals
As thick as hasty pudding."

"Head Quarters, Plymouth, January 23d, 1807.
'Division Orders"

The Division Court Martial, whereof Brigadier General Bates of the Second Brigade is President, is hereby ordered to convene at Mr. Caleb Loring's, in Plympton, on Thursday the 19th of February next, punctually at eleven o'clock A. M.

By order of Major General, 5th Division,
"N. Hayward, A. D. Camp."

"Head Quarters, Wareham, February 6th 1807.
"Brigade Orders"

All persons of the Frst Brigade, interested in the foregoing Division Orders are directed to attend to and obey accordingly."

By order of the Brigadier General,
William Hammett, "Brigade Major."

"Head Quarters, Bridgewater April 10th 1811.
"Brigade Orders"

All the commissioned officers of the Battalion of Artillery attached to the First Brigade, are ordered to convene at Mr. Caleb Loring's house in Plympton, on Monday, the 27th day of May next, at eleven of the clock A. M., to make choice of a Major Commandant of said Battalion, vice Joseph Thomas resigned. Colonel Thomas of the First Regiment, will preside and make return of the election accordingly."

By order of the Brigadier General, 1st Brigade,
William Hammett, Brigade Major.

"Head Quarters April 23d 1811.
"Battalion Orders."

The Commissioned officers of the Battalion of Artillery in the First Brigade, and Fifth Division, will pay strict attention to the foregoing order. Commissioned officers will appear on said day in uniform complete, with side arms." Thomas Turner, Adjutant of Artillery.

"First Brigade 5th Division.
"Brigade Orders"

Captain Noyes Commanding officer of the Battalion of Artillery in said Brigade, is directed to give legal notice to the officers of said Battalion, who by law may vote in the election of Field officers, that they assemble at the house of Thomas B Harrub, innholder, in Plympton, on Thursday the 22 instant, at one o'clock, P. M., for the purpose of filling the vacancy of Major in said Battalion. Given at Middleborough, the Head Quarters of the Brigadier General, and by his order, July 2d, 1824.

"Nathaniel Wilder Jr., Brigade Major."

"Head Quarters, North Bridgewater, July 4th 1824."
"Battalion Orders."

The Commanding officers of the companies of Artillery in the First Brigade, 5th Division, are ordered to appear at Thomas B. Harrubs in Plympton, with their subalterns on Thursday the 22d instant, at one o'clock P. M., for the purpose of choosing a Major.

By order of Captain Moses Noyes, Senior Officer,
Samuel N. Dyer, Adjutant.

This Battalion of Artillery was composed of three companies, viz: the Plymouth Artillery company first organized July 8th 1777. The Abington Artillery company organized December 24th 1787, and the Hanover Artillery company organized May 3d. 1802.

In 1843 these Artillery companies together with an Artillery company in the town of Norton (organized October 31st 1776), were made a regiment of Artillery and at the first election of field officers, Wendall Hall of Plymouth, was chosen Colonel; Daniel Barstow of Hanover, Lieutenant Colonel; and Earl Hodges of Norton, Major. Francis J. Noyes of Boston, was appointed Adjutant. Ebenezer W. Peirce of Freetown, Quarter Master. John P. Wade of Dighton, Pay Master. Levi Hubbard of Plymouth, Surgeon, and Robert B. Hall of Plymouth, Chaplain. August 31st 1844, Ebenezer W. Peirce was promoted to Major of this Regiment, and on the 5th of September 1846, to Lieut. Colonel. Honorably discharged, July 27th 1848. The Norton and Abington Artillery companies performed military service in three wars, viz: the Revoultion, the last war with England, began 1812 and that of Great Rebellion of 1861.

The Plymouth Artillery served the country in the Revolution and war of 1812, and the Hanover in 1812 alone, as it was not formed until after the Revolution, and disbanded before the great Rebellion. Each of those time honored institutions, had interesting histories, but this is neither the time nor place to set forth in their proper order the facts that go to make up the same in detail, and we will therefore dismiss that subject by adding briefly, concerning the Battalion. The Plymouth and Abington Artillery companies, were first made a Battalion in August 1794, and Captain Luke Nash of the Abington Artillery company made Major, and the Battalion organization continued about 37 years, when broken up and the three companies of which it then consisted, were annexed to the 1st 2d and 3d Regiments of the local militia of Plymouth County.

PLYMPTON. 55

During that 37 years that it retained the Battalion organization the following named gentlemen held the office of Major Commandant. Luke Nash of Abington, Joseph Thomas of Plymouth, Micah White of Abington, Moses Noyes of North Bridgewater, Marcus Reed of Abington, and Elias W. Pratt of Scituate.

Three years later these three companies were again made a Battalion and thus remained nine years, when by the addition of the Norton Artillery company it became a Regiment. Majors of the Battalion from 1834 to 1843. William Thomas of Middleborough, from Augu,t 23, to 1834 to 1836; William Pearson of Plymouth, from February 18, 1837 to December 31, 1838 ; Ephraim Holmes of Plymouth, from February 9, 1839 to 1841 ; Daniel Barstow of Hanover, from 1841 to 1843.

Company of Infantry at Plympton, that responded to the " *first call*" of the country in the late war of the "great Rebellion", and served three months at and near Fortress Munroe, in Virginia, it being company H. in the Third Regiment Mass. Militia, under Colonel David W. Wadrop, and in the Brigade commanded by Brigadier General Ebenezer W. Peirce. Commissioned Officers. Lucian L. Perkins, Captain ; Oscar E. Washburn, Lieutenant ; both of Plympton, Southworth Loring, of Middleborough, Second Lieutenant. Non Commissioned Officers. Sergeants ; Ira S. Holmes, Jonathan C. Blanchard, and John B. Wright, of Plympton, and Oliver H. Bryant, of Kingston.

Corporals ; Edwin A. Wright, John Jordan, Henry K. Ellis, and Alexander L. Churchill, all of Plympton. Privates: Josiah E. Atwood, Benjamin S. Atwood, William C. Alden, George B. Bryant, Daniel Blackman, Calvin Benson, Lorenzo L. Brown, Henry F. Benton, George W. Baldwin, Ezra S. Churchill, Frederick S. Churchill, Marshall M. Chandler, Daniel Dwyer, Albert A. Darling, William P. Eldridge, William Fay, Daniel Foley, Francis M. French, Josiah P. Hammond, Frederick Haynes, Seth E. Hartwell, Philander Herrin, Charles H. Jones, Briggs O. Keen, Melvin G. Leach, Lemuel J. Loud, Thomas Morton Jr., Solomon Meserve, Robert Parris, Israel B. Phinney, Edward F. Phinney, Lucian M. Raymond, Seth D. Reed, Warren Rickard, Frank H. Shephard, Michael Shean, Major Tirrell, John A. Fowle, Francis S. Thomas, Alonzo Turner, Samuel G. Thompson, Alva P. Vaughn, Lewis T. Wade, James F. Willis, Rufus F. Wright.

PLYMPTON TOWN OFFICERS.—1873-4.

Town Clerk.—L. B. Parker.

Selectmen, Assessors, and Overseers of the Poor.—John Sherman, Ira S. Holmes Lemuel Bryant.

Treasurer.—Zacheus Parker.

Collector.—A. S. Sherman,

School Committee.—Mrs. R. W. Parker, Miss Nancy S. Loring, Miss Eudora H. Perkins.

Constable.—A. S. Sherman.

Congregational Church.—Rev. Philip Titcomb, Pastor.

ROCHESTER.

This town is said to have derived its name from the ancient city of Rochester, in Kent, England, a shire from whence came many of the first planters of Scituate, Mass.

A committee of the church at Scituate, in 1638, obtained from the Colonial Court at Plymouth a grant of land at "*Scipican,*" for the seating of a township and a congregation.

The territory however remained unoccupied until 1651.

The first white settlers arrived in or about 1680, and were principally from the towns of Marshfield, Sandwich, and Scituate.

It was originally a very large township, but considerably diminished by the setting off of the towns of Marion and Mattapoisett.

Rev. Samuel Arnold, is said to have been the first or earliest minister. He was succeeded by Rev. Timothy Ruggles, who was settled in 1710.

A Baptist church was formed here in or about 1793.

Before the division of this town, and the setting off of Marion and Mattapoisett, Rochester had eight churches, viz., four Congregational, two Baptist, and one Quaker.

Lieut. Colonel Ebenezer White, of this town, performed good service for the cause of his country, in the "days that tried men's souls."

He was commissioned as Lieut. Colonel of the Fourth Regiment Plymouth County Militia, in the first year of the Revolutionary War, and while participating in one of the engagements that took place in Rhode Island, had a part of the hilt of his sword shot off.

In the cemetery at Rochester Centre, or that part called "*Rochester Town*," stands an old brown stone, bearing the following inscription,

"*Memento Mori*, Sacred to the memory of Col. Ebenezer White, who died March 1804, aged 80.

He was 19 times chosen to represent the town of Rochester in the General Court ; in 14 of which elections he was unanimously chosen. As a tribute of respect for his faithful services, the Town erected this monument to his memory."

Elnathan Haskell, of Rochester, was Major of Artillery in Continental Army. His likeness appears in one of the historic paintings that adorn the dome of the Capital at Washington City, D. C.

Major Elnathan Haskell, was chief of the division staff when the fifth division (embracing the local militia of Barnstable, Bristol, and Plymouth Counties), was commanded by Major General David Cobb, of Taunton.

Nathan Willis, formerly a merchant at " Rochester Town," and a very enterprising man, was promoted to the office of Major General of Militia. Hon. Marcus Morton held the office of Judge Advocate on General Willis' Staff.

Rochester gentlemen who have held commissions as Field Officers, in the local militia :

Colonels — Charles Sturtevant, from Jan. 4, 1797, to 1800 ; Noah Dexter, from 1812, to Aug. 5th, 1812 ; David Hathaway, from 1826 to 1829 ; John H. Clark, from December 8th, 1829. Abial P. Robinson, from May 7, 1834, to 1837.

Lieutenant Colonels — Ebenezer White, from 1775 to 1781 ; Charles Sturtevant, from May 1, 1794, to Jan. 4, 1797 ; Noah Dexter, from June, 1809, to 1812 ; Ebenezer Barrows, from 1826 to 1827 ; John H. Clark, from 1827 to Dec. 8, 1829; Gilbert Hathaway, from 1839 to April 24, 1840.

Majors — Edward Winslow, from an early and unknown date. Elisha Ruggles, from 1787, to 17— Charles Sturtevant, from 179– to May 1, 1794 ; Roland Luce, from July 22, 1800, to 1806 ; Noah Dexter, from 1807, to June, 1809 ; Nathaniel Haskell, from 1814, to 1821 ; David Hathaway, from Oct. 10, 1823, to 1826 ; John H. Clark, from 1826 to 1827. Abial P. Robinson, from 1832, to May 7, 1834 ; Charles H. Clark, from May 7, 1834, to 1836 ; Gilbert Hathaway, from 1837, to 1839 ; Rogers L. Barstow, from 1853, to 1858.

Part of a company of cavalry, for several years existed in

town, and and of which Nathaniel Haskell, John Bennett, Ira Clark, and James H. Clark, were successively commandders, Captain Haskell, being promoted to Major of the Cavalry Battallion.

A company of Light Infantry, was raised in 1849, and James H. Look, commissioned Captain. He was succeedd by Rogers L. Barstow, in 1851. This company belonged to the Third Regiment of Light Infantry, then commanded by Colonel Eliab Ward, of Middleborough, and in the Second Brigade Mass. Volunteer Militia, then under Brigadier General Henry Durham, of Abington.

While Marion and Mattapoisett, remained as parts of Rochester, the town could properly lay claim to considerable commercial enterprise, two hundred and fifteen workmen being at one time engaged in ship building.

Whaling was also carried on and the making of salt. At one time about sixty sail of merchant and coasting vessels, were owned here. What by many was believed to have been the most valuable private Library in the State, was owned by Rev. Thomas Robbins, formerly a settled clergyman, in that part of Rochester, now Mattapoisett.

This library consisted of about three thousand volumes and four thousand pamphlets. He also had an extensive collection of coins, manuscripts, &c.

Rochester Company of "*Minute Men*" that responded to the first call April 19th, 1775.

Commissioned Officers. Edward Hammond, Captain ; Josiah Burgess, Lieutantant ; Timothy Ruggles, Ensign. Non Commissioned Officers. Sergeants ; William Nye, Jonathan King, Stafford Hammond, Sylvester Bates. Corporals ; Church Mendall, Elisha Briggs, David Snow, William Crapo. Private Soldiers ; Ichabod Nye, William Randall, Nathan Savery, ——— Bassett, Richard Warren, Nathaniel Ryder, George Hammond, Joseph Clark, Shubael Hammond, Rufus Bassett, Jonathan Clark, Lemuel Caswell, Nathan Nye, Seth Mendall, Moses Bates, Consider King. Hathaway Randall, Seth Hathaway, Elijah Caswell, jr., Nathan Perry, Isaac Washburn, Japhet Washburn, Caleb Combs, Joseph Hammond, Benjamin Haskins, John Briggs, Elijah Bates, David Bates, Daniel Mendall, Samuel Snow, Nathan Sears, Nathaniel King, Weston Clark, Robert Rider, Silas Bassett, Ebenezer Foster, George Clark, William Hopper.

Rochester 2d foot company of *Militia* that responded to the "Lexington Alarm" April 19th, 1775.

Nathaniel Hammond, Captain; Nathaniel Briggs, Lieutenant; John Briggs, Lemuel Le Baron Sergeants; Corporals, Increase Clapp, Samuel Jenness. John ——, Charles Sturtevant, —— Sturdevant, —— Hammond, Joel Ellis, Nathaniel Sears, Joseph Haskell, 2d, Benjamin Dexter, Daniel Hammond, —— Briggs, Samuel Sampson, Ichabod Clapp, Joshua Allen, John Allen, jr., John Clark, Hosea Bolles, John Keen, Jos. Wing, Ebenezer Hammond, Elisha Briggs, Private Soldiers. (See roll at State House).

The 4th regiment in 2d Brigade 5th Division, that from about the commencement of the war of the revolution, embraced all the militia companies of Middleborough, Rochester, and Wareham, were divided in the days of gerrymandering (see order of Governor and Council, at the State House, Boston, Jan. 15, 1812), and the companies of Rochester and Wareham set off, and wish those of Carver, made a new and distinct regiment, of which Major Noah Dexter, of Rochester was elected and commissioned Lieutenant Colonel Commandant. Benjamin Ellis of Carver, Major, and Asa Barrows appointed Adjutant. This was disbanded by order of the Governor and Council August 5th, 1812, and the companies of Rochester and Wareham set back to the 4th regiment, then commanded by Lieutenant Colonel Abial Washburn of Middleborough, Levi Peirce of Middleborough being Senior or First Major, and Samuel White, Junior Major.

From 1812 to 1826, Rochester and Wareham militia continued to form a part of the 4th regiment, and at the date last mentioned was again divided pursuant to the following order.

"The committee of Council on Military Affairs, to whom was referred the petition of Sylvanus Barrows and other commissioned officers in the 4th regiment, 1st Brigade, 5th Division of the militia of this commonwealth, praying, for the reasons therein set forth, that the said 4th regiment may be divided, and that the several companies of militia in the towns of Rochester and Wareham, now constituting a part of said fourth regiment, together with the south company in the town of Carver, now constituting a part of the first regiment in said Brigade, may form and constitute a new regiment, respectfully report that His Excellency be advised to detach from the fourth regiment aforesaid the companies of militia, with their officers, within the limits of the said towns of Rochester and Wareham, and the south company in Carver with their officers, from the aforesaid first regiment, and to form the aforesaid detachment into a new regiment, to be denominated the fifth regiment in first Brigade fifth Division aforesaid, and that such field and staff officers as belonged to the fourth regiment aforesaid, and who are now resident and domiciled within the limits now provided for said new regiment shall retain their respective ranks and be attached to said new regiment. The committee further report that it appears that the field officers of the fourth regiment aforesaid, the Brigadier and Major Generals of the first Brigade and fifth Division, have approved of the petition aforesaid and that no objection appears from the officers of the south company in Carver aforesaid, or from the officers of the first regiment, all of which is submitted by order of the committee."

"In Council July 8th, 1826, Nathan Willis Chairman."
"The above report is considered and accepted, and by the Governor approved,"
"Attest Edward D. Bangs, Secretary."

"Commonwealth of Massachusetts," Head Quarters, Boston, July 14th 1826. General orders. Major General Lincoln of the fifth Division is directed to carry the above advice of Council, approved by the Governor, into effect, and to give the necessary orders for the organization of the new Regiment."
"By His Excellency's Command,
William H. Sumner, Adjutant General."

"Head Quarters, New Bedford, July 17th 1826."
"Division Orders."
The Major General directs that Brigadier General Ephraim Ward of the first Brigade issue the orders necessary for carrying into effect immediately the foregoing advice of Council of the 8th, and general orders of the 14th current."
"By order of the Major General 5th Division,
Timothy G. Coffin, Aid De Camp."

"Head Quarters, Middleborough, July 28th 1826,"
"Brigade Order."
The Brigadier General directs that the aforegoing advice of Council of the 8th, and general orders of the 14th, and division orders of the 17th current be carried into immediate effect.

Lieutenant Colonel Wood, commandant of the 4th regiment will transmit copies of the foregoing advice of Council, General and Division orders, together with this order, to each of the commanding officers of companies in the town of Middleborough, now composing said fourth regiment.

"Major David Hathaway, senior officer of the fifth or new regiment will transmit similar copies to each commanding officer of a company within the limits prescribed by the advice of Council aforesaid, to constitute said new or 5th regiment. Lieutenant Colonel Wood, Major Hathaway, and all others concerned, will take due notice of the advice of Council aforesaid, General, Division and Brigade orders, and govern themselves according to the precept thereof.

By order of the Brigadier General, 1st Brigade 5th Division, Nathaniel Wilder, B. Major."

The field officers in this new regiment were filled by electing and commissioning three Rochester gentlemen, namely: David Hathaway, Colonel, Ebenezer Barrows, Lieutenant-Colonel, and John H. Clark, Major. Doctor Thomas E. Gage, of Rochester, was appointed Adjutant.

Colonel David Hathaway, was born in Freetown, Sept. 24, 1788. He was a son of Gilbert Hathaway of Freetown, and wife, Mary Evans. Gilbert and Mary were married Nov. 24th 1779. She was born Feb. 12th 1751. She was a daughter of David Evans Jr., and wife, Anna Weaver, of Swansey, who were married Nov. 29 1745. Anna was a daughter of Benjamin Weaver of Swansey, and wife, Ruth Sheffield, Benjamin and Ruth were married April 11, 1723.

Ebenezer Barrows was promoted to Lieutenant Colonel from the office of Captain of the Light Infantry company then existing in that part of Rochester now Mattapoisett. He resigned, and was succeeded as Lieutenant Colonel by Major John H. Clark, who finally succeeded Colonel Hathaway in the command of the regiment December 8th, 1829.

The first election for the choice of Field officers for this regiment was held 1826. Major John H. Clark was promoted to Lieutenant Colonel, in place of Ebenezer Barrows. September 11th, 1827, was the time set for the election to be held at the house of Elisha Ruggles, innholder, but this was countermanded in Brigade orders of Sept. 7th, 1827, and Major Clark was not promoted until some time after.

Lucius Downs succeeded John H. Clark as Major, and was in turn succeeded by Stillman Shaw. This 5th regiment existed but a few years, when it was disbanded, and the companies of Rochester and Wareham again became a part of the fourth regiment, and thus continued until the abolition of the old militia system, by an act of the Massachusetts Legislature, April 24th, 1840.

Rochester Justices of the Peace, and date of appointments.
Ebenezer White, Oct. 31, 1775 ; David Wing, Aug. 28, 1775 ; David Nye, May 17, 1787 ; Elnathan Haskell, May 28, 1787 ; Abraham Holmes, March 2, 1789 ; Nathan Willis, March 4, 1800 ; Nathaniel Hammond 3rd, Feb. 19, 1805 ; Nathaniel Ruggles, Jan. 26, 1810 ; Elisha Ruggles, May 5, 1810 ; Gideon Barstow Jr , Feb. 22, 1811 ; Caleb Briggs, Feb. 22, 1811 ; Elijah Willis, Feb. 22, 1811 ; Peleg Whitridge, May 8, 1812 ; Charles J. Holmes, Feb. 15, 1814 ; Micah H. Ruggles, Jan. 31, 1815 ; Thomas Bassett, Jan. 30, 1816 ; Charles Sturtevant, Jan. 30, 1816 ; Joseph Meigs, Feb. 3, 1816 ; George Wing, Feb. 5, 1822 ; James Ruggles, April 16, 1822 ; Jesse Martin, May 26, 1823 ; Joseph Look, May 26, 1823 ; Philip Crandon, Feb. 17, 1824 ; Lothrop Perkins, Feb. 17, 1824 ; Butler Wing, Jan. 7, 1825 ; William Le Baron, July 1, 1825 ; George King, Jan. 24, 1829 ; Theophilus Pitcher, Jr., Feb. 1, 1831 ; David Hathaway, Jan. 12, 1836 ; Walton N. Ellis, Jan. 12, 1836 ; Joseph Haskell, Feb. 7, 1837 ; Joseph W. Church, April 11, 1839 ; Theophilus King, July 25, 1839 ; Noah C. Perkins, Feb. 17, 1841 ; Amitta B. Hammond, March 6, 1841 ; Rogers L. Barstow, Jan. 14, 1843 ; Benjamin F. Barstow, Feb. 12, 1851. James H. Lock, George Peirce, Thos. Ellis.

Coroners. — Nathaniel Haskell, March 1, 1794 ; Peleg Whitridge, Jan. 26, 1802 ; Nathaniel Haskell Jr., June 17, 1815.

TOWN OFFICERS, 1873-4.

Town Clerk, Treasurer, and Collector — Henry C. Nye.
Selectmen, Overseers of the Poor, and Assessors — John Blackmer, George H. Peirce, John G. Dexter.
School Committee — G. B. Blackmer, Joseph E. Church, Henry H. Bennett, L. D. Braley, Charles H. Alley.
Constables — Robert C. Randall, Judah Hathaway, Town Agent, James Ruggles, Herring Inspector, G. B. Blackmer.

CHURCHES.

Congregational Church — Rev. Nelson Clark, Pastor.
North Rochester Congl. Church — No settled Pastor.
Union Church — No settled Pastor.

WAREHAM.

Agawam was the Indian name of this locality. It was sold by the natives in 1655, the town of Plymouth being the purchaser. In 1682 the town of Plymouth, for two hundred pounds, conveyd it by deed of sale to Joseph Warren, Wm. Clark, Joseph Bartlett and Josiah Morton, of Plymouth, Isaac Little, of Marshfield and Seth Pope, of Dartmouth.

The earliest permanent English settlers came from Hingham and chief among whom was Israel Fearing.

It was incorporated as a township in 1739. Their first settled minister was Rev. Roland Thatcher, who was ordained in 1740 and died in 1773. Thus it appears that from the date of purchase to that of incorporation, was eighty-four years. Rev. Josiah Cotton succeeded Mr. Thatcher as the town's minister, and he was in turn succeeded by Rev. Noble Everett, ordained in 1784.

At the breaking out or commencement of the war of the American Revolution, the train bands and alarm lists of Middleborough, Rochester and Wareham were detached and set off from the Plymouth or first regiment in Plymouth County Militia, and made to constitute a new regiment, numbered and known as the Fourth Regiment.

Of this then new Fourth Regiment, Ebenezer Sprout, of Middleborough, who had been Major of the first regiment, was promoted to Colonel. Ebenezer White, of Rochester, Lieut. Colonel, Israel Fearing, of Wareham, Senior, or first Major, and John Nelson, of Middleborough, now Lakeville, Junior or second Major.

Israel Fearing was in 1785 promoted to Lieut. Colonel, in 1787, to Colonel, and in a few years after to Brigadier General.

While General Fearing commanded the Brigade, and Major General Nathaniel Goodwin the Division, Fearing's Brigade was called out pursuant to orders, as follows :

DIVISION ORDERS.

Head Quarters, Plymouth, August 27, 1803

" Brigadier General Fearing is ordered to parade with his Brigade, including Cavalry and Artillery, for review, inspection and discipline, near the widow Dunbar's, in Halifax, on Wednesday, 12 October next, at 9 o'clock A. M., completely equipped with arms and accoutrements and eight rounds of sporting cartridges.

" The Commander-in-Chief it is expected will review the

Brigade, and the Major General flatters himself the officers and soldiers will conduct with that martial spirit, order and subordination which they displayed on a similar occasion."

By order of the Major General, 5 Division.

(Signed)   N. HAYWARD, A. D. C.

BRIGADE ORDERS.
Head Quarters, Wareham, Sept. 1st. 1803.

"In pursuance of the foregoing Division Orders, and to carry the same into effect, the General of Brigade directs the officers commanding Regiments and Battalions in 1st Brigade 5th Division to parade with their respective commands at the time and place therein mentioned. Punctuality is the main spring of military subordination. He recommends that each commanding officer appoint his alarm post so near the parade as to enable him to lead on his command at the appointed moment. For the order and regulation of the day, reference may be had to Brigade Orders 29 August and 9 Sept., 1799, part of which will probably be attempted. If any other arrangements are made they will be seasonably communicated."

Per Order,
(signed)   W. JACKSON.
Brigade Major.

The Brigade then consisted of 4 Regiments of Infantry, a Battalion of Cavalry, and a Battalion of Artillery, and these commands were officered in the field as follows:

1st Regiment, Militia of Plymouth, Carver and Kingston. *John Thomas, Lieut. Colonel Commandant, Zacheus Bartlett, and George Russell, Mayors.

2d. Regiment, Militia of Scituate, Hanover and Pembroke. Charles Turner, of Scituate, Lieut. Colonel Commandant, Nathaniel Sylvester and John James, Majors, and Samuel Eels, Adjutant.

3d Regiment, Militia of Abington and the Bridgewaters. Sylvanus Lazell, of Bridgewater, Lieut. Colonel Commandant, Caleb Howard and James Barrett, Majors, and Hector Orr, Adjutant.

*Colonel John Thomas was from a military stock. He was a son of Major General Thomas, of the Patriot Army of the Revolution, and who perished in the service of his country at Chamblee. The son resided on the same spot of ground in Kingston, that had been the home of his father. Of 1st Regiment, John Thomas held successively the offices of Adjutant, Major, Lieut. Colonel and Colonel. Col. Sylvanus Lazell succeeded General Fearing as Brigadier General. He was the founder of and a large proprietor in the extensive "Iron Works" in Bridgewater.

4th Regiment, Militia of Middleborough, Rochester and Wareham. *Abiel Washburn, of Middleborough, Lieut. Col. Commandant, Peter Hoar, of Middleborough and Roland Luce, of Rochester, Majors, and Cyrus Keith, of Middleborough, Adjutant.

CAVALRY BATTALION.

Companies of Cavalry in Bridgewaters and Middleborough. William Bourne,† of Middleborough, Major Commandant. Elias Dunbar, of Bridgewater, Adjutant.

ARTILLERY BATTALION.

Companies of Artillery‡ in Plymouth, Abington and Hanover. Joseph Thomas, of Plymouth, Major Commandant and William Hammatt, Adjutant.

These three companies of Artillery constituted a Battalion for many years. Disbanded in or about 1831, reformed again in 1834, again disbanded in 1843.

But it was not as a Brigadier General of the Plymouth County Militia that Israel Fearing acquired that notoriety among the people, and the good name for which he was distinguished. The circumstance which caused him to stand forth so conspicuously in the public mind, and to hold so high a place in its affections and such a share in its love, esteem and confidence, was of an earlier date, and transpired during the war of the Revolution, when Israel Fearing had only attained to the rank and commission of Major in 4th Regiment Plymouth County Militia.

---

*Col. Abiel Washburn was a son of Edward Washburn, of Middleborough, (that part now Lakeville,) Edward was a patriot soldier in war of Revolution.

Col. Washburn succeeded Sylvanus Lazell as Brigadier General, Sept. 4, 1816.

†Major William Bourne was a son of Capt. Abner Bourne, of Middleborough, who commanded a company in the Revolutionary war. Major Bourne was a senator from Plymouth County and one of County Commissioners. Died Dec. 10, 1845, in the house where he was born.

‡The Plymouth Artillery Company was organized July 8, 1777, Thomas Mayhew was the first captain. It was disbanded in or about 1850.

The Abington Artillery was organized Dec. 24, 1787.

The Hanover Artillery Company was organized May 3d, 1802. Hon. Benjamin Whitman was the first captain. These companies, together with the Norton Artillery Company that was organized in October, 1776, were brought together in 1813 and organized as a Regiment of Artillery. Wendall Hall, of Plymouth, commissioned Colonel, Ephraim B. Richards, of Boston, Lieut. Colonel, Ebenezer W. Peirce, of Freetown, Major ; Francis I. Noyes, of Boston, Adjutant, Robert B. Hall, of Plymouth, Chaplain ; John P. Wade, of No Dighton, Paymaster.

The story has oft been told, and repeatedly appeared in different publications, and to many of the readers of this article are, perhaps, as familiar as " household words," yet in this connection it seems that to omit it would be inexcusable, and therefore we here present that version of the affair given in " Dwight's Travels," volume 3, page 71, describing the circumstances which attended the attempt made by the British troops to destroy the village of Fairhaven on the night of Sept. 7, 1778, they having previously burned some of the houses and destroyed a large amount of property at New Bedford.

" From this place they marched around the head of the river to Sconticut Point, on the eastern side, leaving in their course, for some unknown reason, the villages of Oxford and Fairhaven. Here they continued until Monday morning, and then re-embarked.

" The following night a large body of them proceeded up the river with the design to finish the work of destruction by burning Fairhaven.

" A critical attention to their movements had convinced the inhabitants that this was their design, and induced them to prepare for their reception.

" The militia of the neighboring country had been summoned for the defence of this village.

Their commander was a man far advanced in years.

" Under the influence of that languor which at this period enfeebles both the body and the mind, he determined that the place must be given up to the enemy, and that no opposition to their ravages could be made with any hope of success.

" This decision of their officer, necessarily spread its benumbing influence over the militia, and threatened an absolute prevention of all enterprise and the destruction of this handsome village.

" Among the officers belonging to the brigade was Israel Fearing, Esq., a Major of one of the regiments.

" This gallant young man, observing the torpor which was spreading among the troops, invited as many as had sufficient spirit to follow him, and station themselves at the post of danger.

" Among those who accepted the invitation was one of the Colonels, who, of course, became commandant; but after they had arrived at Fairhaven, and the night had come on, he proposed to march the troops back into the country.

"He was warmly opposed by Major Fearing, and finding that he could not prevail, prudently retired to a house three miles distant, where he passed the night in safety.

"After the Colonel had withdrawn, Major Fearing, now commander-in-chief, arranged his men with activity and skill, and soon perceived the British approaching.

"The militia, in the strictest sense, raw, already alarmed by the reluctance of their superior officers to meet the enemy, and naturally judging that men of years must understand the real state of the danger better than Major Fearing, a mere youth, were panic struck at the approach of the enemy, and instantly withdrew from their post.

At this critical moment, Major Fearing, with the decision which awes men into a strong sense of duty, rallied them; and placing himself in the rear, declared in a tone which removed all doubt, that he would kill the first man whom he found retreating.

"The resolution of their chief recalled theirs. With the utmost expedition he then led them to the scene of danger.

"The British had already set fire to several stores. Between these buildings and the rest of the village he stationed his troops, and ordered them to lie close in profound silence, until the enemy, who were advancing, should have come so near, that no marksman could easily mistake his object. The orders were punctually obeyed. When the enemy had arrived within this distance the Americans arose, and with a well directed fire, gave them a warm and unexpected reception. The British fled instantly to their boats, and fell down the river with the utmost expedition.

"From the quantity of blood found the next day in their line of march, it was supposed that their loss was considerable.

"Thus did this heroic youth, in opposition to his superior officers, preserve Fairhaven, and merit a statue from its inhabitants."

Major Fearing was also for a time on duty in Rhode Island, and stationed at or near a place called "Fogland."

From this account of the stirring scenes witnessed at, and of what was transpiring in the little village of Fairhaven on that memorable night in September, almost one hundred years ago, it appears that a certain Colonel greatly over-rated himself, snuffing the battle bravely so long as the danger was far off, but proving wholly useless when trouble was near.

That Colonel, if we trust to tradition, became a laughing

stock then, and his conduct the subject of ridicule for many years after.

Half a century later, some personal enemies of Colonel John Nelson of Middleborough, tried to create the belief that he was the cowardly colonel referred to, which any one conversant with the facts must have known were untrue, because impossible, as John Nelson was at that date (viz., Sept. 1778) holding the commission of Junior Major, and was not a Colonel until July 1st, 1781, or almost three years later. He was Junior in rank at that time (1778) to Israel Fearing, and consequently the withdrawal of John Nelson was not necessary to give the command to or make the leadership devolve on Fearing, who at that time was a Senior Major, and consequently Nelson's superior officer.

A veteran soldier of the war of the revolution (named Bennett), a few years since in relating to Mr. Daniel Ricketson of New Bedford, what he remembered of this transaction, said that the poltroon was a Colonel, but Mr. Bennett, like Mr. Dwight, suppressed the name of that officer.

The gist of the matter lies in the circumstance that at the re-organization of the militia in July 1781, a wrong was done Major Fearing, who ought to have been promoted, but was not, but left out of the arrangement altogether.

Junior Major John Nelson being at that time made Colonel. Captain William Tupper of Middleborough *Lieutenant Colonel*, and Captain Edward Sparrow of Middleborough, *Major*. A great deal of trouble resulted from that unjust proceeding, and to make " honors easy" Lieutenant Colonel Tupper resigned, and Israel Fearing was made his successor in (1785), being then of course made Junior to John Nelson, to whom in the war of Revolution, he had been *Senior* or superior officer.

The circumstance that Isreal Fearing was finally John Nelson's subaltern or inferior officer, led those not conversant with all the facts in their cases to suppose such was the positions that they relatively sustained in the war of the revolution, and hence it became easy to make it believed by those who knew no better that the withdrawal of John Nelson from a post of danger naturally, and as a legitimate consequence, threw the responsibility on Isreal Fearing, and that it was John Nelson who thus withdrew.

Amends were made to Fearing for the cruel neglect he suffered in 1781, for he was, as remarked made a Lieutenant Colonel in 1785, a Colonel in 1787, and ere long a Brigadier

General. He stands in history thoroughly vindicated, and there is no necessity for injuring the name or marring the fame of John Nelson, on Fearing's account. If John Nelson was at fault, it was when he allowed himself to be promoted over the head of and to supercede so brave and meritorious an officer as Israel Fearing, and for that let us blame him, but not for a thing of which he was not, and from the circumstances existing at the time could not have been guilty. "Let justice be done, though the heavens fall."

Wareham, in the latest war with England, (or the war of 1812 as it is sometimes called,) suffered an attack from the marines, or sailors of the British war vessels " Superb " and " Nimrod," then blockading the harbors of this coast.

A rocky neck of land of considerable elevation, which conceals a view of the bay from the village, also concealed the approach of a detachment of barges from the British war vessels.

On the morning of June 13th, 1814, six barges, carrying about two hundred men, effected a landing, and although remaining but a few hours, destroyed forty thousand dollars worth of property, by setting fire to one ship and one brig that were in process of construction, (on the stocks,) and burning several schooners and sloops. The fire in the ship and brig was extinguished, and thus these only sustained a partial loss.

Their attempt to burn the cotton factory was not successful.

Capt. Israel Fearing, Jr., (a son of Brigadier General Fearing,) called out the militia, and did all that under the circumstances could be done for the defence of the place. Although not so successful as his father in the former war had been, at Fairhaven, he displayed the same heroic spirit, richly deserving the appellation of "*parentibus optimus bene merentibus.*"

The following named Wareham gentlemen held commissions of generals and field officers in the local militia of the State.

Major General — Darius Miller, from 1833 to 1835.

Brigadier General — Israel Fearing.

Colonels — Israel Fearing from 1787 to ———; Bartlett Murdock

Lieut. Colonels — Israel Fearing from 1785 to 1787.

Majors — Israel Fearing, from 1775 to 1781; Wm. Barrows, from April 20, 1812, to August, 1812; Lucius Downs. Brigade Inspector, with the rank of Major, James Sproat; Aid to Major General, with the rank of Major, Warren Murdock.

The Militia company of Wareham, that responded to the call April 19th, 1775.

Commissioned Officers: Noah Fearing, Captain; John Gibbs, Lieutenant; Non-Commissioned Officers. Jonathan Gibbs, Joseph Sturtevant, Sergeants; Enos Howard, Corporal; Thomas Norris, Drummer; Joseph Bumpus, Joseph Winslow, Jesse Swift, —— Bumpus, John Bates, —— Bassett, Benjamin Swift, Jno. Bourne, Archipaus Landers, —— Hathaway, Samuel Savery, David Nye, Privates.

Company of "Minute Men" from Wareham that marched to Marshfield, April 19th, 1775.

Commissioned Officers: Israel Fearing, Captain; Joshua Briggs, Lieutenant; Ebenezer Chubbuck, 2d Lieutenant; Non-Commissioned Officers. Samuel Savens, Prince Burgess, Edward Sparrow, —— Burgess, Sergeants; Jno. Bessee, Drummer; Joshua Bessee, Fifer; Samuel Burgess, Sylvester Bumpus, Calvin Howard, Wilbur Swift, Benjamin Gibbs, Samuel Phillips, Rufus Perry, Nathaniel Burgess, Joshua Gibbs jr., William Parris, Isaac Ames, William Bumpus, David Perry, Benjamin Briggs, Barnabus Bumpus, Elisha Burgess, Richard Sears, Asaph Bates, Jabez Nye, Jno. Lothrop, Ebenezer Bourne, Willis Barrows, Samuel Norris, Joseph Bumpus, Elisha Swift, Jabez Bessee, Samuel Morse, Thomas Sampson, Timothy Chubbuck, Privates.

The following named soldiers of Wareham, gave their lives as a sacrifice to the Union cause in the late war of the great Rebellion.

First Battalion, Daniel Westgate.

Third Regiment, Joseph W. Tinkham, John D. Manter, John S. Oldham.

Sixth Battery, John A. Haskins, December 6, 1864.

Eighteenth Regiment, Thomas S. Hatch, James F. Leonard, William Ashton, Samuel Benson, Theodore E. Paddock, Arch. Stinger, Marcus Atwood.

Twentieth Regiment, James R. Russell, James Blackwell, Benjamin F. Bumpus, John J. Carroll, Benjamin D. Clifton, James Madigan, Julian W. Swift, George H. Loring.

Twenty Fourth Regiment, George H. French, Stephen S. Russell, Daniel C. Bumpus, Joseph Hayden, Isaac S. Oldham, Feb. 2d 1863, David A. Perry.

Twenty Eighth Regiment, under Colonel Montieth, Patrick Crim.

Fifty Eighth Regiment, under Colonel Whiton, Patrick Cox, Horatio G. Harlow, Stephen H. Drew, George W. Bessey, July 2d, 1864. Not assigned to Regt., John R. Oldham.

Recapitulation. Not assigned, 1 ; 1st Battalion, Company D. 1 ; 3d Regiment, 3 ; 6th Battery, 1 ; 8th Regiment, 17 ; 20th Regiment, 7 ; 24th Regiment, 6 ; 28th Regiment, 1 ; 58th Regiment, 4. Total, 32.

Justices of the Peace, with the dates of their appointment. Isreal Fearing, —— 1747 ; Noah Fearing, January 23d, 1777 ; Isreal Fearing, February 28th, 1798 ; Benjamin Fearing, June 16th, 1800 ; John Fearing, January 31st, 1804 ; Roland Leonard, May 16th, 1810 ; Wadworth Crocker, February 5th, 1811 ; Benjamin Bourne, February 12th, 1812 ; Bartlett Murdock, February 1st, 1819 ; William Fearing, February 11th, 1820 ; Curtis Tobey, February 17th, 1824 ; Seth Miller jr., June 29th, 1826 ; Sylvanus Bourne, August 27th, 1829 ; David Nye, March 12th, 1830 ; Charles E. Ellis, February 14th, 1832 ; Thomas Savery, January 29th, 1836 ; William Bates, March 3d, 1836 ; Darius Miller, March 30th, 1858 ; Harrison G. O. Ellis, September 21st, 1829. William L. Chipman, Joseph P. Hayden, James G. Sproat, John M. Kinney, Adolphus Savery, Nathaniel Sherman, Noble Howard.

Trial Justice. — Seth Miller.

Notaries Public. — William L. Chipman, James G. Sproat.

TOWN OFFICERS, 1873-4.

Town Clerk and Treasurer. — Alvin F. Gibbs.

Selectmen, Assessors, and Overseers of the Poor. — Alden Bessey, Nathaniel Sherman, B. F. Gibbs.

School Committee. — S. B. Bumpus, John M. Kinney, Galen Humphrey.

Surveyors of Highways. — William H. Mackie, John Galt, Ebenezer Bryant.

Coroners. — Samuel Savory, September 20th, 1780 ; Curtis Tobey, February 3rd, 1808 ; Perez F. Briggs, June 11th 1827.

WEST BRIDGEWATER.

Although one of the towns last incorporated in Plymouth County, West Bridgewater is, nevertheless, an early English settlement; in fact it was the first interior settlement of Plymouth colony, and showed marks of civilization more than two hundred and twenty years ago.

Remaining a part of ancient Bridgewater as it did, from 1651 to 1822, a period of one hundred and seventy-one years, its date of incorporation as a new and distinct town causes it to rank as the youngest in the county, save East Bridgewater, Lakeville, Marion and Mattpoisett.

The history of West Bridgewater is, therefore in fact, nearly all a part of the history of ancient Bridgewater.

At the commencement of the settlement, each settler had a house lot of six acres near the river, then called " Nunketest," which name for a long time was applied to the settlement itself.

Rev. James Keith was their first minister. He was from Scotland, and came to Boston in or about 1662, and was ordained at Bridgewater in 1664. Died in 1719 aged 76; must have been born in or about 1643.

This was the first interior settlement in Plymouth County, and its early inhabitants were called on to encounter many and repeated dangers and troubles incident to Indian warfare. During King Philip's war, 1675 and 1676, they displayed great resolution and intrepidity. Surrounded as they were by the savage foe, and strongly advised and solicited to leave their dwellings and to repair to the towns at the seaside, they, however, resolutely held their ground, and successfully defended the settlement and encouraged and assisted some other towns to do likewise.

On the south side of the river they erected and maintained a stockade, and there kept a small garrison. They also fortified several of their dwellings.

Sunday, April 9th, 1676, they received a visit from the indians who burned one house and a barn, broke into, and rifled several other houses, but fled as soon as pursued.

May 8, 1676, the Indians, about three hundred in number, led by Tispaquin, the noted chieftan of Middleborough, paid the people of Bridgewater a second visit, making an assault upon the east end of the town, set fire to many of the English dwellings, but, as said the old chronicle, " the inhabitants issuing from their houses, fell upon them so resolutely that the enemy were repelled and a heavy shower of rain falling at the same time, the fires were soon extinguished."

This was on the south side of the river, and failing in their attempts in that direction, the Indians now repaired to the north side of the stream, where the attack was renewed, but they were again driven off after burning two houses and one barn.

Houses upon the outskirts of the town, deserted by their owners, fell a prey to the Indian's torch, by which fourteen houses four barns, including those in the village, were destroyed.

Sometime, during the summer of 1676, Capt. Benjamin Church, with a body of soldiers, were sent to aid in this defence, and twenty Bridgewater men going out to meet Capt. Church, came upon a band of Indians, of whom they captured seventeen together with considerable plunder. The next day, as a part of captain Church's command, they participated in conquering a tribe of one hundred and seventy-three Indians. These Indian prisoners were taken to Bridgewater, and confined in the town-pound.

The old chronicle adds, concerning the Indian captives: " They were well treated with victuals and drink, and the prisoners laughed as loud as the soldiers, not having been so well treated for a long time."

Tradition informs us that not a single Bridgewater man was slain in that war, nor in any other in which the county had engaged, until they were called upon to participate in the " Old French War," so called, 1745, when John Snell, of B,idgewater, fell in battle.

In the war for Independence, viz., at the capture of Burgoyne, Capt. Jacob Allen, of Bridgewater, was slain.

Comfort Willis, the Bridgewater " Trooper," who figured so conspicuously in " King Philip's War," is said to have kept a diary of those stirring events, as the same were occurring. He was the ancestor of Judge Samuel Willis, of Dartmouth, now New Bedford. Samuel Willis was Colonel [*] of the Second Regiment, Bristol County Militia, in the time of the " Old French War," 1745, and 1746. His son, Ebenezer

---

[*] The local militia of Bristol County were then organized into three Regiments of which Dr. Thomas Bowen was Colonel of the 1st, Samuel Willis, Dartmouth, Colonel of the 2nd, and George Leonard, of Norton, Colonel of the 3rd. A few years later, Daniel Carpenter, of Rehoboth, succeeded Dr. Bowen, as Colonel. Ezra Richmond of Dighton, succeeded Colonel Willis, and Ephraim Leonard succeeded his brother, George Leonard.

Willis, was Major of the same regiment, just before the breaking out of the Revolutionary War.

* A lineal descendant, named Samuel Willis, was Adjutant of the same Regiment, about the time of the "Shay's Rebellion."

Hon William Baylies, distinguished for his ability as a lawyer, (although a native of Dighton,) resided in West Bridgewater, for many years.

Justices of the Peace, West Bridgewater.

Jonathan Snow, Jan. 7, 1824; Samuel Dunbar, Feb. 17, 1824; Jonathan Copeland Jr., June 10, 1825; William Baylies, Jan. 7, 1826; John E. Howard, March 2, 1826; Abiezer Alger, Jan. 2, 1828; Austin Packard, March 4, 1828; Daniel Howard, Dec. 3, 1828; Zephaniah Howard, Feb. 28, 1829; Ellis Ames, March 5, 1835; Linus Howard, June 28, 1836; Jonathan Ames, April 13, 1843; Abial Packard, April 13, 1843; Elijah Smith, April 13, 1843; Dwelley Forbes, Jan. 4, 1848; Joseph Kingman, Feb. 6, 1851; Samuel D. Keith, Dec. 6, 1853; James Howard, William H. Jennings.

Names of West Bridgewater men who died for their country, in the late war.

Second Regiment, John B. Dunbar.

Third Regiment, George Colwell,

Seventh Regiment, under Colonel Darius Couch, Henry Quintley.

Ninth Regiment, under Col. Cass, Patrick Cunningham, Co. K.

Twelvth Regiment, under Webster, Timothy O'Kary.

Twenty Sixth Regiment, John B. Gould, Grenville Howard, Lyman E. Howard, Francis Lothrop.

Twenty Ninth Regiment, under Colonel Ebenezer W. Peirce, Myron E. Alger, Chas. H. Hayden, Chas. H. Turner.

Fortieth Regiment, Charles H. Parker, Asa F. Shaw.

Fifty Eighth Regiment, under Colonel Whiton, Leonard Jones, Henry M. Folsom, Eustace Howard, Hector O. Kingman.

* When the Second Regiment was reorganized to meet the emergencies of the "Shay's War," soon after the close of the Revolution, George Claghorn, of New Bedford, was commissioned as Colonel, Benjamin Weaver, of Freetown, Lieut Colonel, Robert Earl, of Westport, Major, Samuel Willis, Dartmouth, Adjutant, and William Almy, Quarter-master. Col. George Claghorn was naval constructor of the frigate Constitution, or " Old Ironsides," as sometimes called. Lieut. Col. Weaver was born in Freetown, June 25, 1775; died in Freetown, April 23, 1838. He was grandfather to the writer of this article.

Fifty Ninth Regiment, Michael McMurphy.
First Cavalry, Roscoe Tucker.
Second Cavalry, Alvan R. Coffin.
In the Navy, James E. Jacobs, James E. Ryan, Wiiliam Dewyre.
Recapitulation. 2d Regiment, 1 ; 3d, 1 ; 7th, 1 ; 9th, 1; 12th, 1 ; 26th, 4 ; 29th, 3 ; 40th, 2 ; 58th, 4 ; 59th, 1 ; 1st Cavalry, 1 ; 2d, Cavalry, 1 ; Navy, 4. Total, 25.

TOWN OFFICERS, 1873-4.

At the annual meeting, James Howard, Moderator, Austin Packard was chosen Town Clerk ; Selectmen, James Howard, Davis Copeland, Samuel N. Howard ; Treasurer and Collector, George M. Pratt ; School Committee, Perez P Field, Heman Copeland and Miss Irene S. Wood, for 3 years, Eli Wheeler, for one year ; Constables, Eli Wheeler, Thomas P. Ripley. The town voted, 45 to 70, not to accept the act relating to road commissioners. Nahum Packard, W. H. Jennings and Bradford Packard were chosen a committee on the part of the town to procure lecturers in accordance with the terms of the Howard fund, with instructions not to exceed the sum of twenty-five dollars for any one lecture. Highways, $2,500, new roads, $500, schools $3000. school house repairs $200, incidentals, 1200, support of the poor, $800, lectures $100,—total $8,300.

First Congregational (Unitarian) Church. Rev. Frank P. Hamblett, Pastor.

Methodist Episcopal Church, (Cochesett), Organized 1829. Present Church erected, 1844.

Baptist Church, Cochesett Village.

Silver Wave Lodge, No. 134. I. O. G. T. Cochesett Village. Instituted January 5, 1870.

Population in 1870, 1,803.

www.ingramcontent.com/pod-product-compliance
Lightning Source LLC
Chambersburg PA
CBHW020324090426
42735CB00009B/1399